TESTIMONIALS

The story is captivating and so real: It is heart wrenching and tragic, yet inspiring.

Chris Andrews. Principal.
Gympie High School. Queensland. Australia.

This is the best true account of abuse and its affect on a young person's life that I have ever read.

Susan Andrews.
Specialist counsellor for sexually abused Aboriginal
children.

A harrowing, heart warming and hopeful story, told in an authentic voice that clearly establishes the difference between terror, confusion, self blame and reality.

John McClean. Psychiatrist. Sydney Australia.

The Future
IS NEVER SOLD OUT

The True Story of a Child Sexual Abuse Victim.

Told through a shadow of tears

Written by
JEFF HADDLETON

From the diary of
IRENE REBUSTO

Ordering Information:

For orders and inquiries, please contact:

CONTENTS

PROLOGUE

A meeting of experience and compassion.

This book has been written as a joint effort between Irene Rebusto from Mindanao in the Philippines and Jeff Haddleton from Australia.

The meeting of minds

At the time Irene and I met she was nineteen years old, living a subsistence life in a shanty with her family in the highland province of Upper Biliran on the island of Mindanao in the Philippines. She was unemployed and had completed only one semester of college. She possessed little of any value in conventional terms, but value is not always a commodity, value is often ethereal. What is of little value to one is often of great value to another. What Irene had in her possession was a diary of years of abuse at the hands of her uncle and her rehabilitation in the Bitoon Sa Langit Foundation. She recognised it however, as having no more than painful, sentimental, personal value, I saw it differently.

Of our meeting she says, 'I met a foreign man and he became my friend. I opened up to him and told him my story. I told him almost everything. He said he would like to write a book about my life, that it is an important story and should be told because it might help other girls who have been abused and other people to understand what girls go though when they suffer abuse. I offered him my diary, but it took many hours of my time to translate it into English so he could understand it. After that we talked many times for many hours each time. Often I cried. He made me remember things I never wanted to remember; things that hurt very deeply.

I am glad now to have done this. Like talking to my counsellor and telling her what happened to me, expressing my feelings has helped me cope better with life. This book is what he wrote as a result of reading my diary and our talks. The story is mine, the experiences are mine, although I wish they were not. My English is not good, so they have been formulated and rewritten in words that flow more easily so English speaking people can understand them, but the sentiment of the words is mine.

I hope you will think he has succeeded in what he has written and that it will help others to be stronger than me. I hope that other girls who have been abused, and their families, can learn from the mistakes I made. When rapes occur, I hope this book teaches families to support their daughters and not turn a blind eye or turn away from them as I believe mine did.'

ABOUT THE AUTHOR

Jeff Haddleton

Jeff is an ardent traveller who, when he met Irene in Cagayan de Oro, was traversing his way overland to Davao. Irene took him to visit the Maria Christina falls in the mountains near her home above Iligan and during the day, shared her experience. Jeff was moved.

He says of their meeting, 'When I heard Irene' story, I recognised from my own poverty stricken childhood the importance that her story could hold in aiding the recovery of other abuse victims. Although all such stories are very personal, each in its own way has deep implications for victims families and for the social workers and counsellors who deal with abuse victims. Communities throughout the world need help in understanding the trauma that sexual abuse victims suffer.'

Irene did not hesitate in giving me her diary, but initially it was useless as a writing aid, it was written in Vasaya and even when translated the English version was so disjointed and incomprehensible I could not understand the compilation of her words. It was not until I realised that I was reading the words of an uneducated, fourteen year old girl, writing in her second language, under the pressure of extreme trauma, that I could make headway in understanding and compiling it. To achieve the task of writing, however, I needed to draw out and understand the pain and emotion behind the words, I needed personal explanations of her experiences What ensued were many, many hours of what I often felt was torture on my part, but it was necessary so I could extract the depth of feeling needed to tell the story properly. Although at the time I did not realise what was occurring, I think that relating her story to a sympathetic and non-judgmental listener greatly assisted Irene in ridding herself of some of the demons and self-doubt she harboured. I nicknamed her 'Little Lion', you will discover why if you read this book in its entirety.'

Jeff was born in New Zealand, but has visited there only twice in the last fifteen years. After joining the merchant marine at the age of fifteen and spending six years tramping the world, he settled down at age twenty-two in Sydney, Australia. He was married for seven years during which he had two children and now has four grandchildren. He calculates that to date, more than twenty years of his life have been spent travelling.

By age twenty six he owned a Real Estate agency and after selling that joined the insurance industry and became a member of the 'Million Dollar Round Table'. A motivational speaker at many conferences, he eventually formed and co-owned what became the biggest insurance brokerage of its type in Australia.

Selling his share to his partners in 1993, he retired at the age of forty-four, bought a yacht and, after a lunch with friends at the Manly Hotel in Sydney, sailed into the sunset with his long time partner.

After eighteen months cruising the east coast of Australia and another eighteen months backpacking through Central and South America, they returned an embraced their hobby of Latin Dancing. Over the next four years they won many national and international titles and placed sixth in the World Championships. As a mature aged student, Jeff received a BA in Philosophy and English Creative Writing from Macquarie University in Sydney in 2005.

His first book '*From The Belly of the Cow*', uses an account of extensive travels through India to tell of lessons learned in a lifetime of business and travel. '*The Future is Never Sold Out*' is his second book.

FORWARD

This story deals with the heartbreaking phenomenon of abuse of children by members of their own family, uncles, cousins, brothers and more often than not, their father or grandfather, and sometimes both. This is the very personal account extracted from the diary and mind of a child, rape victim during her ordeal and attempt to rehabilitate herself. (A child is defined in international law as anyone below the age of 18 years of age. In the Philippines, they number 32 million, almost 43% of the total population (1999 MICS)). Irene's rapes continued almost unabated through her thirteenth and fourteenth years. This is a more prolonged period than occurs in most cases, but not unique, a fact that makes her story all the more horrific.

In movies we see many depiction of rape, normally portrayed as committed by strangers or occasional acquaintances, but in the vast majority of rapes this is untrue. More rapes are committed by family members or close family friends than by strangers.

Laurence Ligier is a French national who runs the Cameleon Association for abused girls near Iloilo in the Western Vasayas. The Association has three homes that house twenty-five girls each. Ligier says that that of the nine-hundred girls she has treated over the last eighteen years, twenty percent were raped by their fathers. She says, when the fathers appear in court *'they act like it is their right and they own their daughters. In all my years with the Cameleon foundation only one father has pleaded guilty.'*[1]

Rapes are a common phenomenon. As I write these words, there is, at this very moment, a television news broadcast of the arrest, only one hour's drive from Irene' home, of a foreign national for multiple rapes, the multiple sexual abuse of minors, and the torture of his victims. Police suspect that in this case there are many unknown victims and are appealing for them to come forward so charges can be pressed to the maximum. In no way however, does this story deal with incidents of abuse by foreigners or the proliferation of child pornography, nor is this an academic study of sexual abuse. The story herein is a very personal, however to explain the enormity of the problem and place individual cases in perspective, some recognition of the extent of the sexual abuse problem is important.

Statistics are unreliable and usually based on available police records, which are mostly inaccurate and conceal the extent of the problem. Although the following figures are a little outdated, in a conference in Manila, DR. ELIZABETH PROTACIO-DE CASTRO,

---

1   *The Philippine Star.* Thursday April 30th 2015.

a professor of Psychology in the University of the Philippines, and many years director of the Children's Rehabilitation Centre (CRC) in Manila, stated that one in three Filipino children experience abuse …

794 rapes occurred in the Philippines in the first four months of 1997 …

2,393 cases of rape, attempted rape, incest, acts of lasciviousness or prostitution occurred in the first semester of 1999, while the PNP (Philippine National Police) reported only 685.

Abuse of children in the Philippines is rife. Only occasionally are convictions recorded so the questions begs, why do so many cases go unreported and, even when cases are commenced, why are so few convictions recoded against the perpetrators?

Dr Elizabeth Protacio-de Castro maintains that '*the cultural and social stigmatisation associated with rape is a significant barrier to women reporting rape or abuse. Furthermore, women are less likely to report rape if there is little support from their families, law enforcement agencies or the health sector. This means that many, probably the majority of cases, are never reported.*' Dr Protacio-de Castro also maintains a contributing factor is *the Philippine concept of utang Na loob* (Indulgence), *which enabled an elderly American to have sex with seventeen minors in Puerto Galera after he gave their parents money and had their houses renovated.*[2] The

---

2http://www.pstcrrc.org/docs/Surviving_the_Odds

story of Irene Rebusto in this book clearly demonstrates how true many of these reasons are.

Once abuse is discovered, very few abuse victims receive formal assistance or help in rehabilitation. For rehabilitation to occur, the 'Handbook for Social Workers on Basic Bio-Psychosocial Help for Children in Need of Special Protection', says that *'the resilience of the child is an important factor'* [in rehabilitation].

Resilience is generally defined as *'The remarkable capacity of individuals to withstand considerable hardships, to bounce back in the face of great adversity, and to go on to live relatively normal lives.'* ... *'Some view resilience more as an individual trait, a personal attribute, or an inner strength. Resilience depends on one's circumstances. While one may benefit from having this inner strength, one would also need "competence" to handle adversities. Children imbued with a sense of independence and confidence to perform certain tasks are more likely to survive adverse circumstances. Furthermore, children who find coherence and hope in their external and internal world, and who are more or less, in control of their destiny, cope better. This is in contrast to passive children who regard themselves as victims.' ...'A special talent or a strong interest in something can spark this sense of mission or purpose in life. Feelings* [of being] *a part of and at home with something outside themselves—perhaps a musical*

_Finding_Hope_in_Abused_Childrens_Stories.pdf

band, work, peer group, or neighbourhood within schools, religious, and community organizations among others—allow them to have a sense of direction in life. Likewise, the ability to see humour in a situation helps them deal with difficult situations.'

The Cameleon Association uses physical activity as a prime form of rehabilitation and therapy. As Laurence Ligier explains *'Sports and physical activity play an integral role in the education and personal rehabilitation of the children at Cameleon.'*[3] To this end they have developed a close relationship with circus trainers from France who train the girls. Cameleon now boast its own circus.

According to Dr Elizabeth Protacio-de Castro, religion also plays its part. Many victims of abuse ask, *'If there is a God, how could He/She allow this to happen to me?'*

Many though *'learn to accept what happened to them, and see their experiences as part of God's plan for them to become stronger persons.'*[4]

According to *'Breaking out of the Glass Cage'*, an article published on March 8th 2015 in the 'Philippine Panorama', a publication of the 'Manila Bulletin', *'ninety percent of the women and girls who came* [to The Coalition Against Trafficking in Women - Asia Pacific], *were abused as children by men known to them - a*

3*Cebu Sun.* May 4th 2015.
4Ibid

father, uncle, a cousin, a neighbour [and], *as society blames rape victims rather than the male perpetrators, the women and girls internalise the guilt.'* The article goes on to say that women are targeted because many men consider women to be little more than sexual objects and convenient commodities.

Another article titled *'Share your love'* in the same publication states that in 2014, 6,011 new cases of HIV were recorded in the Philippines, placing it among the top eight countries with increasing numbers of people living with HIV.

Statistics and analyses are a tool in understanding in the treatment of abuse, but they do not tell of the pain, anguish and fear, or of the destroyed minds: they say nothing of the dehumanisation victims feel or their inability to trust or again have faith in their fellow man again. The question then begs, after eighteen months of continual abuse, what would Irene Rebusto's mind be like? Can she recover? Could anyone recover? Where is she now? Did she wind up a prostitute on the streets or a drug addict? Has she been committed to a mental home? Or did she go to the other extreme and find solace by embracing religion? All these are options to traumatised minds.

GLOSSARY OF TERMS

CDO	Cagayan de Oro city in North Mindanao. Philippines.
Davao	City in South Eastern Mindanao.
Iligan	City in North Mindanao.
Zamboanga	City and province in Western Mindanao.
CR	Comfort room (Combined toilet and washroom).
Load	Prepaid, pay for use telephone account.
Jollibee	A fast food outlet.
Adobo	A style of cooking using soy sauce as a base.
Agta	Small black forest spirit with long hair and pointed teeth
Antinganting	Also *Agimat*. Amulet/charm. Protection against spirits.
Asuwang	Mythological vampire-like beast that can change shape.
Ate	Big sister.
Agus 6 & 7	Electrical plants at dams in Upper Biliran.
Bahala na	Fatalism or resignation. A come what may attitude.

Barangay	Suburb.
Beadle	Assistant.
Bitoon Sa Langit	Shining Star E.G. Shining Star Foundation
Buko	Coconut.
Calandaria	Small, local, food stall and general store.
Chicharon	A crispy junk food made from deep fried pig skin.
Ekog	Tail.
Gaba	A folk religion of the Vasaya islands of the Philippines.
Kasing	A spinning top.
Lubot	Backside or Arse.
Maalaala Mo Kaya	Recalling the memories.
Malata	Suitcase.
Manananggal	A human bird that sucks foetus from pregnant women.
Maya bird	Sparrow.
Mga Bata Foundation	Many Children. E.G. Many Children Foundation.
Munchkins	Bite sized cake made from biscuits and coconut milk.
Newang	Skinny.
Ningas Cogon	Attitude of, good in the beginning, but not continuing.
Otin	Male reproductive organ. A penis.
Pandan	A fragrant leaf (like bay leaf) used in cooking.

Patintiro	A game like tag played with teams of three or four.
Polis	Police.
Sala	Living room.
Sari sari store	Small general store.
Sigbin,	Type of spirit or witch in the form of a long eared dog.
Sipon	Snot
Song ka	A game played with a dice and shells.
Sundang	Machete.
Taba	Fat.
Taxi	A childhood game.
Tikbalang.	Type of spirit or witch that s half human and half horse.
Tita	Auntie.
Totoy	Ladies breast.

NB.

All names have been changed to disguise the identities of anyone who might be harmed, embarrassed or recognized by their inclusion in this book.

The Name of the Bitoon Sa Langit Foundation is not the true name of the foundation where Irene Rebusto was confined for five years.

There is no Upper Biliran in Mindanao

All personal details and details of Irene' experiences are true as perceived by the storyteller and understood by the author.

NB.

Bringing order out of memory

When you read this book you will encounter grammatical errors. They are purposeful for the following reasons …

1 … When Irene was raped for the first time she was thirteen years old and was still in elementary school.
2 … When she started her diary she was sixteen years old and had completed only one year of high school.

3 ... The original diary was written in Vasaya because English is her second language. 4 ... When Irene interpreted her diary into English, the erratic nature of her mind at the time meant there were a large amounts of repetition and an erratic relationship between time and incident. Incidents were not written in any chronological order making it very difficult to determine sequence, verbiage was excessive and the grammar jumbled to say the least.

5 ... Much of the verbiage has been eradicated and the grammar simplified, however, for the sake of authenticity and, to try to convey the range and depth of feelings experienced, I have attempted to maintain the voice expressed in the translation of her diary and our conversations. It does not therefore always read as fluently as educated writing should. Some grammatical errors and a hopefully unburdening amount of repetition have been intentionally included for the above reasons.

CHAPTER 1

The Rape and Rape of Irene

November 2006

When I was two years old my family moved to Davao coz my father was confined to the hospital there when he could not pee. My grandmother and grandfather also moved to Davao to look after me. When my grandparents went back to Upper Biliran in the mountains behind Iligan, I went with them and stayed in their house. They were my grandparents on the side of my father and they cared for me. I was three years old when we returned so I do not remember much about this.

When my father got well, my parents moved to Bukidnon for a while before coming back to Upper Biliran, but they had nowhere to live. A friend of my father had a spare lot of land and let him build a small house there to live in. It was close to the big shed where he stored the coconuts they burned to get oil for cooking. Nobody lived near that house because it was deep in the forest. At night there were only lamps, coz no electricity came to that place. Even the water had to be carried from the well a long way away. The house was very small; only three people could lay down in there. When I was about ten years old my Grandfather decided to share some of his land with his children so my father built a place across the road from his parents. This house was big, it measured five metres by four metres and had two rooms so now my parents had a room to themselves. Mostly it was made of wood, but there was bamboo on the floor and in the windows. We would cook on a fire under a coconut tree and bathe in the communal washing area under a corrugated iron roof that would blow away every time there was a big wind. To go to the CR we had to cross the road and use the one behind my grandparent's house. Our new house was big enough for all us children, there were six of us by then, and my mother's parents as well, so with my parents we were ten. At night time it was very crowded when we all lay down, but we were a family and we all lived together.

Many times I didn't like to go to school. Each day I had to walk more than three kilometres on the dirt road to get there and another three kilometres to come home and when it rained the road got very muddy. I went to school in Biliran from grade one to four, then came a war to our place. Many Muslim people live in a town called Marawi close to Upper Biliran and they made a lot of trouble. The authorities were afraid they would blow up the dams holding back the lake and all the water would wash down the Tambakan River and destroy Iligan city, so the army came and told us we must move from our house. For one month we lived at an evacuation centre in the elementary school. At this time many other families lived there coz there was much fighting between the Muslims and the army. Many times we would see shells flying over the school. When they landed they made a big BOOM and there would be lots of smoke. After one month the fighting stopped and the army told everyone it was safe to go home again.

My auntie Nona from Aurora in Zamboanga Del Sur was worried and said she would like to look after me coz I was a sickly child, so when I was about ten or eleven, I was sent there for two years and lived with auntie Nona through grade five and six.

Auntie in Aurora was very good to me, she treated me like her own child, like I belonged to her. She would take me to the park where we could play, she sent me to school so I could learn and she brought everything for me that I need. After school I would help her sell vegetables and small things from her *sari sari* store in the markets. I loved Auntie Nona; she showed me what a real mother is like. My real mother did none of these things. She never cared for me like a real mother. Auntie Nona would take me to her family farm where they grew corn and coconut trees and vegetables. Together we would clean the house of her niece who lived on the farm with her four children. We worked at cutting the grass with a scythe and we would gather wood for cooking. She taught me how to eat with a fork and spoon coz I never done that before. In our house we ate in the traditional way with our fingers only. Together we did all the jobs that needed to be done and Auntie Nona made me feel like I am part of her family. She never told bad things to me or scolded me, always she tried to help me understand what is good and how to do good things and I always felt I was cared for. At home my real mother never talked to me, she would send me away while she tended to my siblings; she never cared for me like a real mother. I was very young then so I did not understand that everyone is not so caring as Auntie Nona.

After two years I chose to go back to upper Biliran because this is my home and this is where my family live. I wanted to study high school in Iligan with my friends. My auntie Nona wanted me to stay in Aurora with her. I think now that if I stayed with her I would never have experienced what happened to me and my childhood would have been good. I chose wrong.

Today my parents still live in that house in Upper Biliran. It seemed big when I was young, but it is small and crowed, it is made of wood and when the wind blows it comes through the holes between the woods, and when it rains buckets are used to catch the water that comes through the roof. Ten people lived in two rooms and we slept on mats on the floor.

My family treated me very different than Auntie Nona. Because I had not grown up with my brothers and sisters I had different expectations to them and placed different values on what is important. I argued with my sister and my mother so much that when I was twelve they moved me across the street to live in the house of my grandparents. My Grandparent's house was beautiful, it had posters of Jesus and Mary and the crucifixion on the walls and I was so happy coz for the first time I had a small room of myself and for the first time I even had a bed for me to sleep in.

Soon after I moved there a man moved into the house with us. My parents told me it was my uncle Freddy from Manila. This was very strange for me because I didn't know I had an uncle from so far away. My grandmother told me he had run away to Manila when he was fifteen because he did bad things at that time. A long time later I heard he ran away because he had sex with the wife of his brother and she got pregnant, but I didn't know this then.

He had a wife who lived in Tungawan in Zamboanga Del Sur so I don't know why he came to live at our place, but he stayed with us in the house of my grandparents. I did not like my uncle, all the time we would fight coz he was always hurting my younger brothers for no reason. My brothers jobs was to take care of our grandparents goats, cows, chickens and pigs, but sometimes they would play instead of doing their work and my uncle would get mad and hit them. Sometimes he would hit them just because they went to the house of our neighbour to play. I did not like him, but after some months he changed. Suddenly he became very friendly to me and my older sister and our friends. He would play volleyball with me and take care of me, he cooked food that I especially liked and started doing nice things like that. I was surprised that he was suddenly being so nice, but still I did not like him. He had a butterfly haircut, like someone put a pot on his head and cut around the edges. He was short and stocky and had thick lips, and when he talked his eyes never looked at you always you felt like he was lying at you.

In November 2006 my grandmother was attacked by high blood pressure and got confined to the hospital two hours away in Iligan city. After three days my grandfather contacted my nun auntie who lived in the city, to find out the situation with my grandmother. I call her my nun auntie coz she is my auntie and she is a religious nun of the Catholics. He used my phone because my sister gave me a phone and I am the only one who had a cell phone at the time. They found out my grandmother was OK and would soon be released. Everybody was very happy at the news, so that night my grandfather and my uncle and my cousins got very drunk. They were still drinking at 10:30pm when I went to my room and went to sleep.

While I'm sleeping I am not aware that my uncle goes inside my room and he has bad plans to me. While I'm sleeping he took off his clothes and then he woke me and did bad things to me. I fight him. I am punching and kicking, but he wins coz he is very strong. He sexes me and he gets my virginity and made me feel very hurting in my private parts. He makes me feel so scared also, coz when he finished he holds me down on the bed and says that if I tell to anybody what he did, that he rape or abuse me, he will kill me. I feel so scared, only thing I want is to get away from him, so when he let me go I get up and while he is still kneeling I kick him in the stomach and I run into the room of my grandfather, but my grandfather doesn't know what happened and he can't hear me when I'm crying. He doesn't hear anything and he doesn't wake up coz he is so drunk. Only thing I can do is sit in the corner of his room and cry and cry so much.

While I am crying I am hurting in my private parts between my legs, but in my mind I'm hurting more coz I am thinking I can't tell to anybody what happened coz my uncle said if I tell to anybody what he did he will kill me. I am confused and so scared, I don't know what to do, my mind won't work. Never could I believe anybody would do this to me, especially my uncle, I am his own niece. I am lying in the room of my grandfather and so crying and so scared and not knowing what to do. All I can think is that it is much better if I keep my mouth shut in case he might kill me. I don't want to die so soon in my young age.

After two hours of staying in the room with the door locked of my grandfather's room, I go out and check if my uncle is still there. When I go in my room my uncle is gone. Now I am sure to lock the door so he can't go inside. I crawl onto my bed, but I can't sleep coz I am so scared to him. I can't believe what just happened. I think maybe I am just dreaming, but I know I am not, coz my private parts is hurting so much. All night I am crying out of my mind, but I must have fallen asleep coz when I woke up it is light. I see blood on my sheet and I start to cry again. I want to hide. Never do I want to see him. I don't want to see anybody so I stay in my room with the door locked, but my sister is calling to me.

She is saying, you need to get up and wash the clothes of the family and do all the chores what you need to do.

When I go out in my room my uncle is sitting down in the *sala* and he is watching me so angry. In my body I am so much hurting and in my mind I feel so much scared so I just walk straight and pretend that I'm not seeing him, but my tears is starting falling down in my eyes. I cannot stop them flowing until I am there in my parent's house, but no-one sees me crying. My mother and my father are gone to work and my brothers and sister are going to school already. I am not going to school at that time, I had to stop, coz my mother had another baby and it is my job to stay home and take care of my little sister.

In the house of my parents I start washing all the clothes and cleaning the house. I cook food for lunch so my younger sister can eat, but while I am doing these I am not seeing that my uncle is outside and he is watching everything what I do. I am trying not to think, I want to keep my mind blank so I arrange all the clean clothes in our room, but while I'm doing this my uncle comes inside and grabs me and pushes me on the mat. He is touching my chest and my private parts and he start to kiss me all over my body. All the time I am crying and struggling to get away from his face. I am shouting him to stop, but he is very strong and I can't move my body coz he holds my hands very tight. He starts pulling my clothes off. Now when I am trying to shout I can't, coz he is pushing his mouth on my lips. His sweat and saliva is dribbling onto my chin and his breath is choking me, then suddenly he stops coz my younger sister is coming in the room and she starts to crying. When he lets me go I dress up and pick up my sister. We are both crying and my tears is making us so much wet coz I can't stop, and while I am crying she can't stop also.

My uncle is watching me and making angry faces, but after awhile he goes back to the house of my grandfather and leaves me alone. When my brother comes home from school I am still crying.

'What happened?' He asks

When I tell him what my uncle did, Jerome gets so angry. He says he will tell to my father, but I say 'No.' I not want to let him tell anyone coz I am scared of my uncle and his words that he will kill to me.

'Relax.' I say 'Don't worry. Now maybe he will stop hurting all of you, and if he doesn't stop, I will tell to mama and papa what he did.'

Jerome is eleven years old and my uncle is always hitting him and hurting him a lot. When I say this to Jerome and talk about my plan to tell mama and papa, my brother gets quiet and relaxes his anger.

My uncle left me alone from that time on and he also stopped hurting my brothers so I didn't tell anyone. I wanted to tell, but I was too scared that if I did he will kill me. and I am only thirteen years of age. I don't want to die in my young age

After three months I am turning fourteen and I feel good and fine. He didn't touch me anymore and I feel like I am recovering from what he did, but one day he comes into my room and pushes me onto the floor, he puts his hand around my throat and holds me very tight and he sexes me again. When he finished he is laying on top of me so I can't move. Over and over he is saying, 'If you tell anyone what I am doing I will kill to you.'

Now it is start again. Almost every day he sexes me. I can't get away coz always I have to be in the house to look after my baby sister. Nobody can hear me when he comes coz all my family is at work or school and when he grabs me he pushes a shirt in my mouth and ties it around my head so I can't shout or make any noise. He pushes me on the floor and is holding my hands over my head so I can't move and when he is finish he lies on me and holds my neck so tight that still I can't move and I can hardly breathe, then he waits until he is ready and then he do it again and again. Days and days he does this. One time he wants to put his *otin* in my mouth, but I cover my mouth and I cry 'No. No'. I close my mouth tightly and shake my head from side to side to hide from him. I just want to die. He doesn't care what I feel or how much my tears is flowing, but he cannot make me open my mouth; I will not let him do this. He treats me like an animal, like I have no feelings, like I am dirty and worth less than a sick dog or a pig or a chicken. Day after day he makes me feel dirty. Sometimes he grabs me in the house or sometimes under the banana trees, even when I am looking after the animals still he does it to me and he is not even care if I have menstruation. I feel like I'm not even human. I feel like I am just some rubbish for him to use. I am not a dog or a chicken, I am not pig, I am a human being, I have feelings you know, I am not an animal: I am a human being.

I feel so ashamed, coz even the pigs and chickens is cared for, but not me. All the time, so many times he rapes me like that and I cry and I hate him, but what can I do. He is strong and all the time he is saying, 'If you tell anyone, I will kill you.'

Many times my Grandparents is in the next room, but they do nothing. How could they not hear me struggle when he is sexing me? I don't understand why they do nothing. I am thinking maybe they do nothing coz it is their son doing this and he is the brother of my father, but when I think like this there is more scared coming inside me coz if they know and they do nothing, then maybe he will never stop. I don't know what to do and I can't say anything coz if I tell anyone, he say he will kill me. This he tells me all the time.

Then one day I get sick in the morning and I start to sometimes get hungry for different foods and I feel very strange inside. I never know that I am pregnant, so I am confused. I not think it is possible that I can get pregnant coz every time my uncle kisses me I am so careful to wash my teeth and my mouth very carefully. I know how girls and women get pregnant coz I see it all the time on TV, the boys and girls are kissing each other and then she gets pregnant, so every time he put his mouth on mine I wash my mouth very careful. How can I be pregnant? I think it is not possible for me to get pregnant, but my uncle knows about this more than me and he knows that I am pregnant.

'Here, you need to drink this tablet' he tells me.

He gives me a tablet, but I am scared to take it. I don't know what kind of tablet it is or what it is for. I think maybe he wants to kill me.

'Why?' I ask him. 'Why I must take that one?'

He will not give me a reason. 'It is good for you and you must drink it so you will feel better.' This is all he says and he stands over me to make sure I drink it.

I drink it without saying anything coz I am scared of what he might do to me if I don't. Two times every day for four days I drink that medicine until my stomach starts hurting very much. Then some blood comes to my private parts. Still I don't know what is happening to me. I am only fourteen years of age and I do not know anything about getting pregnant or having babies or abortions. When I saw my mother kissing my father, she got pregnant, but when she has my little sister she went in the birthing centre so I do not see her make the baby. I know nothing about how she does this.

There is no glass in the windows of our house, only shutters that get closed when there is raining. All the time mosquitoes and bugs and sometimes birds come in if they want to. When I was pregnant and I was in my room alone one night, the shutters was open and I see something outside my window. It is sitting on the roof of the CR and it is black - very black. It is sitting there and its eyes are watching me. I don't know if this one a man or woman or animal or what, but it has a strange shape like I never seen before so I think it is *Aswang*. Aswangs are like witches, when they want they can change themselves to become half human and half bird. At night they fly around and swoop down on people. You can hear them when they fly coz they make a sound like wok-wok-wok. Sometimes they can change into other types of animals like horses. I cannot hear the wok-wok sound, but I'm very scared so I run to the room of my grandfather. This night I sleep with him there coz I am very scared of that *Asuwang* one.

After I drink all those tablets and start bleeding I know I am pregnant. Now I am full of guilt for the bad things I have done. I am so young to be getting pregnant, and so many mixed emotions I feel coz now I have killed my baby. I don't want the baby of my uncle, but my guilt makes me very scared. What if the police come to arrest me for killing my baby, what would happen then? I am scared coz now maybe the neighbours will be thinking bad things of me. Also I am scared of God coz he might punish me for making a sin and doing this abortion. I am scared of my uncle, I am scared of the wok-wok, I am scared for going to bed at night in case my uncle comes in my room, I am scared to wake up in the morning coz then I am alone in the house, I am scared for everything and I am alone with my scared and don't know what to do.

I am fourteen years of old and now I don't care what happens of me. I don't care anything of myself because after he abort the baby he continues what he do to me and I can't stop him. I hate him, and I hate myself so much coz I am so dirty and so scared. I'm just an animal and he uses me all the time. Every day he do this to me coz my parents is working and my siblings is in school. I am there in the house alone coz I am the only one to look after my baby sister. He doesn't care if I am crying and feeling weak or sick. One time was so bad, when I was having fever my body is going hot and cold and my skin is sweating and very wet, and still he sexes me. He doesn't care if I am sick or having fever, he doesn't care I am crying and feeling so weak, he doesn't care for anything of me. He is not even thinking I am human. All the time my uncle is sexing me he does not allow me to do anything. He is not allowing me to watch TV with my cousins, or talk to any of my friends who is boys, always I must stay in my room. My skin is getting dry and I am getting so skinny. Now I am so small.

On May 3rd there comes a fiesta in Upper Biliran. My grandparents always celebrate fiesta time so all my relatives and cousins and aunties and neighbours gather at the house of my grandparents to cook *lechon* on the spit. All us children are playing many games and my uncles and my father is drinking and getting drunk. Now for a little time I have freedom for bonding with my cousins. We are laughing together in the KTV videoke place of my neighbour and my childhood friend, but when my uncle sees us having fun he stops drinking and comes to my friend's house. He is very angry and he calls to me to come outside. He is shouting that I am not allowed to talk with my boy cousins. He makes me very frightened with his angry and his shouting, but there are many people around so I walk away, but he follows me. Now I am very afraid. I don't want to be alone with him so I go back to the videoke bar where my cousins are having fun. My cousin Adot is sitting in a chair and when I come back he grabs my shirt and pulls me and I fall down onto his knees. When my uncle sees this he comes inside the videoke bar and he is blowing like a big storm. He grabs my hair and pulls me outside and all the time he is shouting at me. I am scared, but there are many people and they are all watching. I think he cannot hurt me in front of all my family and friends so I shout back to him. When I shout to him he is very surprised that I would dare to do this, but I am very surprised too coz suddenly he punches me hard in my stomach. I am so shocked and I fall down on the dirt. Tears is coming to my face. I am crying so loudly and so very much and I cannot get my breath. This is the first time anyone is hurting me like this.

Now he has hurt me I am more scared of him, but what makes me even more scared is that he punched me in front of everyone, my father and my grandfather and my cousins and my neighbours and nobody did anything to stop him. I know I am nothing to my uncle and now, when I see nobody doing anything to help me, I understand that I am nothing to my family also. Now I am scared of everyone. Now I know that even if I tell my parents what he all the time does to me they will do nothing to help me.

I run to the house of my grandparents and hide in my room. My mind is talking to me over and over. It is saying 'you are stupid. You cannot protect yourself and you cannot even summon the courage to talk to anyone. You are on your own and now you know nobody will do anything to help you.'

I feel so lonely. My insides feel like there is nothing there. I keep asking myself. 'What am I to do now?' I cannot avoid him, I don't have confidence to tell anybody what my uncle is doing, and now I know that even if I did tell them they would do nothing to help me. The knowledge that nobody will help me keeps going around and around in my mind so much it makes me dizzy sick. In the corner of my room I curl into a little ball and cry and cry until I fall sleep.

Sometime in the night I move my hand and feel something is wrong. It is dark, I cannot see, but I become aware that someone is on my bed with me. I see my uncle is lying naked beside me. When I move he put his hand across my mouth so I can't make a noise. He holds my throat very tight and he pulls off my clothes. I am so scared and crying coz I can hardly breathe and he is hurting me so much. Then he pushes himself inside me and rapes me again.

Many times he does this, for many months. Even in the same night he does this many times. Every time I see him in the daytime or in the night my body is sobbing so much. All the time I am so afraid. I can't control my tears and I do not know what to do. All the time he is telling me he will kill me if I tell my parents or my grandparents, and now I know that they did not protect me when he punch me in the stomach in front of everyone, I know it is no use to open up to tell them what he is doing.. For more than one year he is doing this, then I get luck. He finds a job in the electricity plant at the hydro-electricity dams of Agus 6 and 7. He is a welder and he goes working there for three months.

Now I have a big time to think if I can tell anybody what happened. But the fears inside myself is very strong that he will kill me. Even if he is not there I'm afraid to tell anybody so I just do all my chores what I have to do and stay quiet.

One day when I am cooking food for my grandparents, my cousin Adot calls me to go to his room in the underground of the house of my grandparents. When I get there he asks me to go buy for him some cigarettes. I go to the store to I buy them, but when I come back he grab my hand and pulls me down on him. At first I think he is just fooling around, but then he holds my arms tight and kisses my lips. I am very shocked. I jump up and pull away and run back to the kitchen. My mind is confused. I cannot think. All my mind can do is tell me to keep cooking the food for my grandparents, but all the time my face is crying. He lives in the room under my grandparent's house so he must hear what my uncle is doing to me all the time. If he hears this and says nothing and doesn't help me, then he must think he can do the same.

What does he think I am? What do all men think I am that they treat me like this? Do they think I am an animal and only here for them to play with like a toy or a dog? I am not an animal. I am not. I keep saying this to myself, I am not, but all the time I am cooking my mind is going out of my body with shock at what happened. Adot is my cousin, I cannot understand why did he would do this to me?

After I finish cooking I go to my room and I start to write in a book all of that has happened in my life. While I am writing, my grandfather calls me to come to the *sala* so we can eat together, but Adot is there so I don't like to eat. I don't want to see him. I continue writing, but my tears are so much like rivers on my face that the paper gets wet and I cannot write anymore, so I go to sleep.

I do not go to school, but my friends do and one of the local schools is having a musical pageant so I ask if I can go. My cousin Jaymark is visiting from CDO and says he will take me, but it is the rainy season and while we are on the way it starts to rain very hard.

'Quick, run to the shed and we will wait for the jeepney there,' he calls. There will be no jeepneys until the rain stops, but it doesn't matter, usually the rain only lasts for a short time, like thirty minutes or so. When we get to the shed the rain is so heavy we cannot see even across the road. We both are very wet, but in the shed there is no rain. Jaymark takes hold of my hand and I think he is going to help me get dry, but he pushes me on the floor. He grabs both my hands and holds them behind my back and starts pulling off my clothes. I fight and scream, but the rain is so heavy and the noise from the rain is so loud that nobody can see or hear me. He rapes me there at the side of the street on the floor of the jeepney shed. When he is finished it is still raining very heavy, but even in the rain I run away to home. My legs is running: my clothes are soaking wet and my hair is tangled around my neck and getting in my eyes, my chest is heaving with sobbing and I cannot get my breath, I cannot understand why he would do this to me. Why does this thing happen to me? What have I done to make this happen? I am trying to think, but all I can feel is the big cloud of sadness surrounding me that is burning and making a pain in my chest. All I wanted to do is go to the musical pageant, but now I am sitting in a puddle of water in my room and I am crying and I cannot stop. My life is worthless, I must be so disgusting that other people must think of me as nothing but an animal coz everybody treats me that way. How can I stop this? I cannot escape, I have no money, I have nowhere to go and I am afraid of everything. He is my cousin, how could ever he do this to me. Now I am afraid this cousin will kill me also like my uncle is always saying he will do. I am afraid now of all the people in Upper Biliran. I feel that I cannot trust anyone. They are all relatives of my father so they are relatives of mine too, but my father's relatives are all bad. They rape my life from me and they think this is alright because nobody will do anything to stop them.

Next day cousin Jaymark goes back to CDO. Sometime later one of my friends told me he came to Iligan because he killed a man in CDO. Then I hear that he gets caught by the police and they put him in prison for this murder what he committed. When I hear this I feel glad this happen to him.

Now my mind is not in my head and I cannot control all the sorrow in my life. I decide to tell to my eldest cousin coz she is a woman. I tell Maria Fe everything that happened with my uncle. She listens and then she tells me that I need to leave and go far away from our place.

'Yes.' I say 'and I want to go straight away, right now.'

She tells me to go pack my things, but while I am doing this she goes up the road to my parent's house and tells my mother what happen to me. Maria Fe lives only five houses down the road so it is not very far, but when I return to her house to get money for my fare, my mother is there. She is crying and she grabs to my hair and starts shaking me.

'Why didn't you tell me what was happening?' She is shouting. She wants me to tell her everything that happened, but I cannot talk, my tongue is like a monster in my mouth and it won't move. 'Tell me what happened.' She is shouting and she keeps shaking me and pulling my hair, but my tongue is swollen and frozen coz of fear. I cannot say anything. She is scaring me and I am weak and I am too afraid of my uncle to say anything. I am not strong enough to talk to them, all I can do is curl up on the floor to protect myself and cry. She is crying also while she is shouting so much to me. 'Why did you stay in the house of your grandparents?' she screeches. 'Why did you not come home to our house? We know that your uncle is bad.'

My mother grabs my hair again and she is pulling it and jerking my head from side to side while she is shouting to me. I try to hold onto her hands so it will not hurt so much. I try to answer, but I cannot answer coz my voice is drowning in tears and my mind is confused and gone into a cloud. If they know my uncle is bad, why did they let him stay with me? Why did they never tell me until now that he is bad? My tears are flowing and I cannot breathe. I feel so weak, but I struggle and fight and when I get free I run and get my things. I want to go far away from there right now. I have no money, but still I run anyway. I run from my mother and I run from my home and I run from my fear, but my fear is too strong and too fast. While I am running my fear is holding on and choking my throat like the hands of my uncle and it will not let go.

I cannot understand why my mother is mad to me. I did nothing wrong. I am not the one who did the raping of me, and now my mother makes me afraid of her. I feel so weak, but I run away until my legs are so tired, then I walk to the house of my god auntie Nanay Trina near the *Barangay* hall. She is the sister of my mother and I know she will tell my mother I am there, but I don't know where else to go. I ask from her money for a fare to go to Aurora to my aunt Nona.

Next morning Nanay Trina gives me the money and as soon as she does I run down the street and catch a jeepney to the bus terminal in Iligan. I will go to Aurora in Zamboanga de Sur. I think I will be safe if I stay with Auntie Nona coz I stayed there for two years when I was in grade five and six and she was treating me like her real child. She cooks for me and care for me and she is looking after me, not like at home, here many times I cannot eat properly coz there is no food and all the time I am being sexed and nobody cares or helps to me.

It is hot in Iligan, but all the time I am waiting for the bus my body is shaking and shivering. Many hours I wait, but the bus doesn't come. Then the father of my childhood friend who owns the KTV karaoke bar, his name is Alex Danyer, he comes to the terminal to get me.

'Uncle Dan, I don't want to go back to that place, let me go away.' I am crying very much when I say this to him, but never won't he let me leave. He gets me back to Upper Biliran and says I will stay in his house for awhile. All the way back into the mountains I cry. I am so scared of my family now, and also I am very scared coz I know it is time for my uncle is finish work in the electrical plant at Agus 6 and 7, soon he will be coming back to our place and maybe he will kill me now that I have told someone what happened to me.

I stay in Alex Danyer's house with my friend for four days. My parents are mad at me coz I ran away. They want me to come home and live in their house, but I refuse. My uncle has returned and he is living across the road with my grandparents again. I decide that never again will I stay in the house of my parents or my grandparents while my uncle is there. After four days Alex Danyer says my father and mother know what my uncle did to me and my grandparents know, and my uncle has run away. Then I agree to go back to the house of my grandparents.

My grandmother called to my nun auntie in Iligan to tell her about what happened, and in a few days she comes to our place to fetch me and take me to her house at Palagan, in Iligan city. I stay with her for awhile, but when I'm there I am so bored. I am the only one in the house, coz nun auntie is always going to the church to pray. I cannot even go out coz she locks the gate. Only thing I can do is climb the mango tree and feel the air. When I was young at home I would climb the mango trees, and coconut trees and banana trees to get the fruit. I am the only one who could climb the banana trees holding on with just my hands and feet.

When I am in the mango tree at my nun auntie's house, the air feels so clean. It feels like the breeze takes all my dirtiness and blows it away for a while. In the mango tree I dream I am a bird and my mind can fly. I would like to fly away, to travel and live in another place, even in other country. In the mango tree I feel a little bit special coz my dreams don't seem silly. Everything feels better and looks better from up here. Sometimes I get some fruit if it is ripe enough to eat, even the fruit tastes better when I eat it in the tree, but all day every day I am alone in the house of my nun auntie and it is very boring, so I decide to go back to our place in Upper Biliran.

The day before I am to leave my nun auntie asks if I am pregnant. I don't want to tell her that I was pregnant from my uncle, or that he already aborted the baby. 'Don't worry,' I say. 'I am not pregnant to him and I am very relieved. If I am pregnant to him I could never accept that child. I would give the child away to someone or I would have an abortion.' I say to her this, coz this is how I feel. I do not mean to upset her, but when she hears these words my nun auntie looks so shocked. She tells me that she wants to send me to school, that I should stay here with her, but I refuse. I cannot do this. I could not live in her place because she always goes to the church for praying and she leaves me alone, here I am so lonely. 'I do want to go to school,' I tell her, 'but I want to go to school in our place with my friends. I am very determined about the way I say this and my words are so strong that she does not contest me.

Next day I wake up early and pack all my things. I wait for my nun auntie to finish her morning prayers, but when she is done, she says that before I go, there is a visitor coming who wants to talk with me. Her visitor is a nun also. She talks some things about God and gives some advice to me that I should be a good girl and continue my study. She says I should I move on from what happened and focus on improving my mind and forget about what happen to me. All the time she is talking I am thinking she is crazy. She has no idea of how abused I feel in my body and all the pain I feel in my mind. My body can recover, but my mind will never forget what my uncle done to me? When she is finished talking she leaves. I call to my nun auntie in her room to say goodbye. She is crying. She says she is sad I am leaving and she hugs me. I know that I am safe here, but I am not sad to be leaving.

I leave at 6pm and arrive home at 8pm. I always climb the mango tree there in the house of my Nun auntie so I bring some mangos, and in the market I buy fish with money my nun auntie gave so I have some food for my family coz many times there is no food in our house. Now I stay in the house of my mother because my uncle is back in the house of my grandparents. They tell me my uncle wants to talk to me. They say he wants to know why I tell everyone that he did bad things to me. He says it is not true.

He is a liar, but I cannot say this to him coz I am too scared to talk to him, but I am more scared of my parents, coz I cannot believe what I am hearing from them, that they don't believe me. I am a child and they know already that he does bad things. How could they think I could make up something like this? I didn't even know about things like sex and rape when he did this. All day every day I stay inside in the house with my mind full of fear again coz I think my parents will not protect me, even now when they knows my uncle is bad. All the time I stay inside our house and if I see my uncle coming I run another way coz maybe he wants to kill me.

All the time I try to think about why this happened to me and what I can do to get away from this place. My uncle raped me, and my cousin rape me and my other cousin kissed me, another cousin is always touching me and my mother and father won't believe me. All the family of my father is bad and I cannot understand why all these things has happened. I feel like I don't belong here and if I cannot belong here then I feel like I cannot belong anywhere. Why are all my family so bad?

I find out that my uncle Jonnelasio, the brother of my father who is living next door, he tried to rape my cousin Marga Mae when she is only five years old, but she is was too young and he couldn't coz she cried too much. When I learned this I realised why he was always pushing himself against me and touching me when I was young. I thought nothing of it then, he is my uncle, I trusted him coz he is my family and I am a child for him to protect. My family knows he tried to rape Marga Mae, but they did nothing to protect me or any of us children. Then he went away to work in a church for some years and we did not see him anymore.

In June 2007 I go to the hospital in Iligan with my mother for a medical exam and the doctor tells me I am too skinny. My weight is 36 kilos. We go to the police station in Iligan to make a warrant against my uncle, but he hears that I am working a case against him so he runs away somewhere. I don't know where.

In June 2007 I started school again. My elder sister Tina Ten takes me to school every day and takes good care of me.

While I am studying, the teachers know what happened to me, but not the students. I sit in the front next to the teacher coz sometimes in class my mind is going away and getting lost somewhere into a big cloudy blackness place. Sometimes I don't even know where my mind is and my teacher has to call me back to attention. After class she talks to me sometimes and asks what is wrong: what happened to me?

I tell her, but while I am talking about my experiences I am thinking she cannot really be understanding what I am saying coz always I am crying too much and my words sound like they are just bubbles coming through my tears. My teacher advises me that whatever happened to me in the past, or whatever happens to me in the future, that I should never be committing suicide. I think she is worried because always I am alone and I don't like to talk to anybody. I like to be alone, but when

I am alone I don't know what I am doing. Sometimes when I am missing she finds me sitting and staring in front of me, but there is nothing there, all I see is a big blackness place and always it is empty.

One day my nun auntie calls my father to say I need to stop my studies. She is worried that no one can protect me at school because my uncle told her he wants to get me and take me far away with him. When they tell me I must stop going to school I get very mad. 'No. I want to finish my studies' I tell them. I continue to my studies until I finish first year high school, then I get a job doing all around everything jobs for my neighbour. I move into their house and live there and this is a good time coz I feel safe with them. Whatever she wants, I do, cleaning the house, washing the clothes, baby sitting and anything else she wants. I know how to do the works that they want so I am busy and nobody yells or gets mad to me. On the weekends I am free. These are my days off and I can do what I like. I can play with my friends and go with them to the mall and have fun hanging out. Always I feel different to my friends, but sometimes when we do these things together I feel like a real person again.

My salary each month is 1,500 pesos, but when I have to pay for my project at school, I have no money coz I give it all to my mother so she can buy food. I text to my nun auntie to ask if I can borrow some money from her and she says it's okay, but I have to come get the money from her place. I get dressed and go with my friends to Iligan. They are going there coz they also need to by some things for their project. We travel together, but while we are in the jeepney my nun auntie texts to say that she is going to my house now and she is bringing someone with her who wants to talk with me. The jeepney is already approaching the city when I get this message and I want to spend time with my friends so I text to my auntie that I cannot go home right now. I am near the city and my friends want me to accompany them to buy some things for their project. 'Much better you give the money to my grandmother and I will get it later when I am back' I say.

For many months I have been texting to my auntie saying that I want to go away. I don't like to stay at home coz Upper Biliran is a darkness place for me and I am always scared. I tell her all the time that my neighbours say I am a bad girl coz my uncle raped me. I tell her I am must always stay in the house coz of the fear I have of going out. Now she replies that she may be able to help me. She says I need to be at the home of my grandmother that night at 7pm.

In Iligan we spend some time trying on dresses and shoes and new jeans, but we can't buy any coz we have no money. All day we laugh and have fun pretending we are dressing up to celebrate our birthdays. My friend's birthday is on July 30th, the day before mine and they are coming soon, but all the day in the back of my mind I am wondering what my nun auntie is going to say when we meet tonight, and who is her friend who wants to talk to me.

When I get to my grandfather's home that night she introduces Sister Claire and she asks of me a favour. She wants to stay there in the house of my grandfather and she wants me to stay with her so we can talk.

'OK. I stay with you,' I say

When we talk she asks me to tell her everything that happened when my uncle was there. 'You need to share everything and not leave anything out,' she tells me.

We spend almost six hours talking and I share to her everything, but I asked her not to say anything to my nun auntie. Sister Claire says, 'But your auntie wants to know what happened to you. She wants to understand. I will call her so we can all talk together and you can explain to her what happened.' But when my nun auntie comes in, Sister Claire gets so confused coz I get very angry at my nun Auntie.

'Why are you so angry at your auntie?' Sister Claire asks.

'Coz I told her what my uncle did and she doesn't believe me. And coz all the time she is blaming me and telling me I am a bad girl and she helps my uncle. When I went to the *barangay* captain and started to make a case against him, she told my uncle what I am doing and he ran away. All she wants to do is protect my uncle and she thinks nothing of me. She believes nothing I say.'

I am talking to Sister Claire when I say this, but my nun auntie is in the room. She hears everything, but she says nothing, only thing she does is sit quietly and play with her rosary beads.

When she leaves, Sister Claire and I talk for a long time more. She wants me to share everything, so that night we talk for more than six hours until after 1am. I am so falling sleepy at that time she says we will finish, but also she says I must sleep beside of my nun auntie and I must give her my phone coz she want to keep it while she is there.

She wants to keep my phone!!! This is a problem for me. Sometimes I receive calls in the night from my friends and I think she will not like this, but I have no choice. She takes my phone and I sleep beside my nun auntie. In the morning my nun auntie goes back to Iligan, but Sister Claire stays for three days. The first night we talked. On the second day she takes me to the *barangay* hall to record to the barangay captain that my uncle raped me. Then we go to DSWD, that is the Department of Social Welfare and Development, to make a report. Then we go to the police station to record everything what happened to me and apply for a warrant for the arrest of my uncle so the police can start processing all my papers. When we go home on the second night Sister Claire stays sitting in our house talking to my mother, but I go outside to join my brother and my friends. They are having drinking near the mango tree with my cousin and making much happiness and fun, but when I walk across the field to join them I hear the wok-wok-wok sound of the witch.

When I hear this wok-wok-wok I run away, but they call to me.

'Don't run' they shout. 'If you run when you hear that wok-wok sound the witch will chase you.'

The boys tell me that if you hear this wok-wok-wok sound going very fast it means that the ghosts are so far way, but if you hear this wok-wok-wok going slow, it means that the witches are close near. The wok-wok-wok we are hearing is very fast so it means the witch is far away, but I am very scared this time coz there is so many types of witches in the forest. My brother's friends tell me that living in the mountains is some *Manananggal*. This one is only half human. At night it grows wings and flies away and swoops down on people and can suck the babies out of pregnant girls like the Asuwang. When it flies away it leaves the bottom half of its body behind. They say you can kill it by putting salt on the body, then when it comes back it can't join together to its body and when the light comes, it dies. Another one like this is called a *Tikbalang*, it is half human and half horse. Also there is a *Sigbin*, this one is a long eared dog and if it bites children they die coz it drinks their blood. In the darkness place in the mountains of Upper Biliran there is many things to make people frightened.

My elder brother and my friends tell me about these ones coz they are boys and they know about these things. They say the only way to have protection from these things is to wear an *antinganting*, but nobody has one of these coz they don't know where to get them anymore. Only very old people can know where to get these ones.

In the morning of the third day Sister Claire and I go back to the police station with my mother because I have to sign many papers. They are so high and so many and all of them are in a big folder. We wait a long time for the warrant of arrest to be issued and released so I can have a copy and the police will have one too.

The police search for my uncle, but they can't find him because my nun auntie told my uncle about the warrant and he run away again. This time I heard he went to another island called Cebu.

Sister Claire stays at our place that night, but next morning she returns to Cagayan de Oro city. She must attend classes at College coz she is taking a degree course in Social work.

I go to school for two more weeks of October then, I stop because I am busy doing more papers for the case against my uncle. First the *barangay* captain and my mother take me to the hospital in Iligan for a medical. I am very shy and embarrassed to have this one, but the doctor is very nice. She says that when I was a virgin, my virgina had lots of numbness coz there is a kind of tissue that covers it. She says that once it is broken it can never come back. After my medical we take the report to the DSWD, then go to the *polis* to sign more papers. After some days when all this is done my nun auntie comes to collect me. She says she will take me to Cagayan de Oro to the house of Sister Claire.

We leave at 9am. During the rides my emotions are very mixed up and confused. I am excited, so I am texting all my friends to say goodbye coz I am moving to CDO for a year or maybe more, I don't know for how long, maybe even for many years I will be gone. I am feeling very alone coz I don't know when I will see all my friends again. I am confused coz I do not know what will happen when we get to Sister Claire's house, but I want to feel safe, this is the most important thing to me right now and I feel I will be safe there. I feel that Sister Claire knows what to do and will do the right thing to help me, this makes me happy. Along the way my nun auntie asked me to turn off the phone. She makes me very upset with these words. 'Why do I need to turn off my phone, for what?' I ask

She replies to me, 'Now your life will be new and nobody from your old life should contact you again. You should stop texting all your friends.'

'But they are my friends,' I say. 'I never stop communicating to all my friends.'

At 3.30pm we arrive in Patag, Carmen, at the house of Sister Claire. She shows me all through the house and to a room where I can sleep and introduces me to her housemate, another Sister Claire, but after one hour she goes to her College to meet all her classmate to do her project. I stay with her flat-mate Sister Claire. She is 31 years old and skinny and she studying psychology, they both are in the final year. Later, Sister Claire brings me to her College to meet her friend ate Maricar who is staying in a foundation and together we go to a Cathedral to attend 6pm mass.

After some days Sister Claire takes me to visit her sister. She says I must stay with her while she goes back to Upper Biliran for my parents to sign some papers that they give their permission for me to enter a foundation. At this time I do not know I am to go to a foundation, I don't even know what a foundation is. I stay in the house of the sister of Sister Claire and her family is very good to me, but I am very shy so I stay in my room all the time. Even when it's time to eat I don't like to leave my room. My shy makes me stay the whole day in my room until Sister Claire is back there.

On 1st of November Sister Claire takes me to visit her parents in Maigo, in Lanao Del Norte where we are to spend there one week. We arrive at 1pm and Sister Claire introduces me to her parents and they are such a good and kind and caring family. Her mother treats me like her own child and cares for me. At that time I have menstruation so she buys me some panty pads. She cooks some food for the family and she shares everything with me at the table just like I am her real daughter. 'Don't be shy,' she says. 'Eat. Just feel like you are at home,' but she cannot know that at my home many times there is nothing to eat.

We spend one week with Sister Claire's parents, then on November 8th, 2009 we go back to CDO again. At 6.30pm Sister Claire tells me that we need to visit some place to see if I would like to stay there. I have no choice. I do not know where she is taking me, but I trust Sister Claire so I accompany to her. We ride a jeepney along the highway until we get near the border of Cagayan de Oro city. Sister Claire presses the doorbell of the Asebido compound of the Bitoon Sa Langit Foundation and a woman opens the gate and tours us around. There are many girls there. She introduces me to some of them, but we have no time to chat or get to know each other. I am confused. My mind is a little numb and not working properly so I cannot understand what this place is, all I know is that lots of girls live here. After we say goodbye and we are in the Jeepney going home, Sister Claire tells me that tonight I must fix my things, because tomorrow I will move to the foundation and stay with the girls. She says that in this place I will be safe. Now I am more confused, nothing seems real. I feel like my head is full of cloudiness and not working properly. I did not know what arrangements Sister Claire would make for me and now I do not know what to think so I keep my mouth shut until we arrive back at the house.

All through dinner we eat without talking. When I am finished I go to my room to pack my things. While I am doing this Sister Claire comes to the room and asks a favour to me. She asks that all my personal things, like my phone, sim card and my ring, that I leave these things with her because these things are not allowed in the foundation. I don't have any choice so I give them to her, but I ask a favour of her also. I ask that she never give my things to my nun auntie. If my nun auntie got these things I would not be comfortable. She is always telling me that I do bad things, like wearing shorts or texting or going to mall with my friends. She wants to control me and I don't trust her to keep my things safe and give them back to me. Sister Claire agrees, but there is one thing I won't leave with her. After she goes out of the room, I get the diary containing all the things that I have written about my life till then and I put it in the trash. If I am going to the foundation I don't want anyone to read what I have written in there. I don't anyone to find out what happened to me and think bad things of me.

CHAPTER 2

Prosecution and Capitulation

November 2009

I visited the foundation on November 8th. On November 9th I move into the foundation. Sister Claire took me there at 3pm. The housemother guided me to my room and gave me my needs like shampoo, bath soap, toothpaste, toothbrush and things like that.

That night all the daughters gather in the dining area to eat dinner. I am very shy. I don't want to go out of my room to join them for eating dinner, but ate Maricar calls me and says I need to eat coz it's the rule of the foundation that all the daughters must eat at mealtimes.There are thirty-five girls in the foundation. All of them sit together at three big tables, but there is no room for me so they allocate me a seat with the staff. After dinner, ate Maricar introduces me to the daughters, then we all go to the chapel for evening prayers. After prayers our housemother introduces me to the daughters again and each one is saying some words of welcoming things. I don't know why these girls are here. I don't think they are like me in my experience so I feel like I am different, I am shy to be among them. This is the first time I experience something like this so I do not feel comfortable and even I their words are nice, I do not feel welcome.

The next day in the afternoon the housemother tells everyone there is to be a meeting for the daughters and we must all go to the productivity room, but the housemother does not know there is already a meeting happening there with the staff and the priests and the board of the foundation: they are watching a movie. When we enter the room we come in behind them so the Priests and the board do not see us standing at the back of the room and for awhile we watch the movie with them.

The movie is using actors, but you cannot see their faces coz they made some fuzzy over them. There is many girls in the movie and all of them have been raped by their fathers or grandfathers or stepfathers or uncles or cousins. When I start to understand what we are watching my body goes cold and my insides start flowing away. There is nothing inside me, I feel hollow and weak, there is nothing to hold me up, but I cannot fall, I feel like I am and frozen in place. The room is not a room anymore, it is a black cloud, and it is sucking all the breath from me and filling me with hurt. I want to sit don before I fall, but I can't do either because I am frozen in place. Then some of the frozen starts melting. My face is wet and my tears are running like monsoon rain from my eyes. This film is about me and all the things that happened to me. I don't want to watch, but my eyes feel like they are stuck to the screen with Mighty Bond and I can't tear them away. I see myself in this movie. It is not me on the screen, but inside it is me coz everything that happens in this movie was done to me. I see the girls being held down and raped. I see the beatings and the threats. I see the hurt and pain and confusion, I see their eyes full with fear. I want to turn away, I want to run away, but a spell has caught me, my body is like ice, I am frozen and cannot move. Only my eyes are moving, they are crying for all the girls in the movie that are suffering like I suffered, like I am still suffering.

I know what it is like to suffer, suffering has been my life for two years now. I know that the pain I see on the face of these girls is nothing compared to the pain in their heart. I know their confusion and insecurity and the loneliness and fear that fills their mind so much it will not work. I cannot move, but I can hear. My eyes will not turn away from the screen, but all around me I can hear the tears crying from the eyes of the other girls. Then Atty Grace is coming and when she sees us she stops the movie.

'Come,' she says. 'All the daughters must leave. You are not allowed to watch this movie.' But it too late, already we saw it.

I feel so bad. I cannot even describe how bad I feel. Everywhere around me is a dark and lonely place and my head is lost in that place. The darkness and the lonely are heavy and they hurt. My legs are walking with the other girls, but I cannot see where I am going. All I see is the darkness in my head, all I can feel is hurt inside. I am crying so much the tears are choking my throat. I cannot breathe. All the girls are the same with their tears,: none of us can stop crying.

On November 16th and 17th one of the social workers from the foundation takes me for an appointment at the hall of Justice in Iligan to meet the Piscal. He asks me to explain everything that happened so they can write it down in an affidavit. He explains to me that on November 20th there will be a court hearing to decide if there is to be a trial and if the other side asks questions, I must answer them in the same way as what is written in the affidavit.

While I am waiting to make my affidavit my auntie comes and she takes me in her arms and she hugs me. I am still mad at my nun auntie, but I am lonely and there are lots of people. I have fear of these people that I do not know and she is a familiar face so I am glad to see her. When you are afraid, it feels good to be held by someone you know, even if you do not like them. My nun auntie has helped me so I am glad to feel her holding me, then I look over her shoulder. Suddenly all the blood goes cold in my body. I struggle to break free. I want to scream. I want to run, I don't want her to touch me, but she holds me very tightly. I struggle harder. I push her and try to run away, but her friend Nanay Belen from the church where my nun auntie goes, she is there and she holds one of my arms to stop me. Now two of them are holding me, I am struggling, but I can't get free. My heart is on fire with fear, it is burning, my chest is heaving, but my body is cold like ice. My eyes are exploding they are so big with fear. Behind my auntie is standing my uncle.

Why is he here? Why did she bring him? Why are they holding me like this when my uncle is there? Do they want him to kill me? My afraid is very big, my body is very cold, my mind cannot think, only there is a dark cloud of fear and its cold grip is holding both my arms. My nun auntie says she wants to ask a favour of me, she wants to talk to me about my uncle. I am shivering so much and my fear is so great I can hardly hear her voice, but some words I hear. She wants me to stop the case. Now my darkness cloud is confused. My uncle did bad things to me. She knows this. Why does she want me to drop the case? I don't know what to say. I can't speak: my voice will not come, fear is blocking my throat. It is so dry I want to scream, I am trying to scream, but no noise will come. A counsellor from the Hall of Justice takes me into a room to talk to me. She asks me what happened, but I can't talk. My tears are flowing down my throat and choking me, but they are sharp like sand and they grate in my throat, they make my tongue swell up and hurt. I cannot make words. When I try to speak it hurts from my mouth to my heart.

In the Hall of Justice there are three counsellors, they all come to ask me what happened so I can make my affidavit, but to none of them can I talk, only tears will come, but no words. The words cannot escape my fear. My uncle is there and if I tell them what happened he might kill me. I want to run away, but I can't. I want to tell them what happened, how my uncle raped my life away, but I can't. I want him to be punished for what he did, but I can't make the words for the affidavit coz my throat is so swollen and my mind is swirling like a black cloud in a typhoon. I am too afraid.

After the third counsellor leaves, the Piscal tells me that my nun auntie told him that what I said against my uncle is not true, that I am making it up and she wants me to drop the case. When he tells me this I pull my legs up to my chest and I hold on to myself so tight. My heart is breaking in my chest and my tears are flowing so much on my face. How could my nun auntie believe this? How could she believe that I would make this up a story like this? I am just fourteen years old. I was thirteen years old when he raped me. How could she think that I even know about things like this to make them up? When the Piscal asks me if I want to continue with the case or not I can't answer him, I don't know what to do. The Piscal decides I must have thirty minute talk and consult with my uncle, just him and me alone in a room. I do not want to do this coz I am very scared of him. I do not want to be alone in a room with my uncle, but if the Piscal says so, then I must.

One of the counsellors takes me in the room. I sit very far away behind the desk trying to stop my body from shaking. When my uncle comes in and closes the door I pull my legs up on the chair, I put my arms around them and try to hold on, but my hands are shaking so much they will not hold on. I cannot look at him, but I cannot look away in case he tries to hurt me. My skin feels cold and stiff and crawling all at the same time, like I am covered in the skin of a snake made of ice and it is glued to my body, but my scales are melting, they are running so much water down my face and it won't stop. My uncle comes close. I try to shrink into a little ball in case he tries to touch me. I want to run away, but I can't coz the Piscal says I must stay here for thirty minutes. My uncle puts his hand on my hand. His touch is like the bite of a poisonous snake. I have never been bitten by a snake, but I think it feels sharp and makes you want to pull back like an electric shock. When he takes my hand it feels numb, like when my tooth broke and the dentist gave me an injection. He says he loves me, but his voice is hoarse and raspy and the words spit at me as sharp as razors, there is no love in this sound. He says he wants me to drop the case, that after I drop the case he will get my number and one day he will come and get me and take me away and we can go somewhere far away. He says I can stay with him and we will live together. He is speaking softly, but words drip from his mouth like green drool from a dog with rabies and roar in my ears. He is sitting so close his smell and his breath are suffocating. I remember these disgusting smells from the many times he holds me down and lies on top of me, they are the smells of evil. Vomit chokes my throat. My body is frozen cold, but my face is running with sweat. My blouse is stuck to my back. I am freezing and melting at the same time.

Is he mad? Can he not see the fear cringing in front of his eyes? No, he is rabid and he is evil, he is a man and he sees only what he wants to see. My mind is a storm of dark clouds and rumbling thunder, but his voice cuts through them like a shard of lightning. I try not to hear his words. I don't want to hear anything he says. My stomach feels like a knot of cassava with all the water squeezed out, it hurts so much I can feel myself shaking with the hurt. All the time he is in the room I cry and I cannot stop. I am so scared. Even when the Piscal comes back I cannot stop crying.

When the Piscal comes back he tells my uncle to go outside, then my nun auntie comes in the room. Again she asks me to drop the case against my uncle. I want to ask her why, but now she is the devil to me, she is doing evil and taking sides with my uncle and my voice won't talk to her.

I don't know what to do so I ask the opinion of my mother, but she won't help. 'It depends on your decision,' she tells me. Now I am very confused and I cry more. I feel that it is wrong to drop the case and let my uncle be free. What about me? I have hurting inside. For two years now I have been hurting. I am scared of the daytime, I am scared of the night time, I am scared of being alone, I am scared of my family, I am scared of everything, but most of all I am scared all the time that my uncle might kill me.

Now my stomach feels like it is boiled dry, all the water has evaporated into my eyes and flowed out in tears, the cassava has combusted and all that is left is ash and charred cinders. It hurts. I don't know what to do. Everyone wants me to drop the case, but I feel that if I do I will always be scared. What if my uncle comes for me and my parents let him take me away and he rapes me again? What if he kills me? I want him to go to jail for what he did. Maybe if he is in jail I won't feel so scared, but everyone is making me feel so much guilty for doing what I feel is right.

At 3pm the social worker takes me back to the foundation. On the way she tells me that my nun auntie said to her that I am sick. She said it was me that tempted my uncle, that I am a bad girl for tempting him and my nun auntie knows this is right coz my uncle told her that I sent text messages to him.

'I not do that. I am thirteen when and he raped me of my young age.' I am yelling at the social worker and now I start crying again. My heart is breaking that anyone could believe such lies. All the way back to the foundation I am sobbing. 'I was thirteen when he raped me' I tell her. 'At that time I not even know what rape is. How could anyone believe that I could do that?'

When we get to the foundation I go to bed and pull the sheet over my head to hide under my shell. I don't want anyone to see how much my tears are crying.

Next day we go back to the Hall of Justice again coz the Piscal must know if I will sign the papers to stop the case or not. My nun auntie is there and again she asks me to stop the case. One time more I ask the opinion of my mother and once more she says, 'it's up to you.' She will not give me advice to drop the case or not. I am very confused. Now I don't know if I am doing the right thing bringing the case against my uncle. I think that maybe I am wrong, coz if I am right she would help me with this decision. I want to bring the case. I feel my uncle should be punished for what he has done, but they don't agree and I am too confused to know if I am right or not. Why does my mother not help? She is older than me so she must understand these things better than me. Why does she not help me? I don't understand.

My nun auntie is talking to me again. Now she is talking about the family. She says she would not like to see one of her brothers put in jail coz it would make the family very embarrassed. My mind screams at these words. What about me and my embarrassed? I am a young girl and all my friends and everyone where I live knows my uncle raped me. When I play with my friends I have to pretend to be a happy young girl like them and nothing bad happened to me. When she says this I feel very hurt and confused. She is like my uncle, she has grabbed me tight in my mind, and she has pushed my mind to the floor and is holding it down so I cannot move. She is chocking my mind. She has ripped it open and is thrusting her will into mine.

I am angry, but I feel like I have no choice. Her family is my family also and I do not want to bring shame to my parents and my siblings. I hate myself for being so weak, but I sign the papers that will I drop the case. The Piscal is very nice. He is very understanding and says I can reopen the case against my uncle any time in the next twenty years.

When you are young you believe in justice and fair play, it is what they teach at school. When we leave the Hall of Justice my emotions are very mixed up confused. I do not feel like my nun auntie or my mother are honest or fair to me and I do not feel like there has been any justice. Night has fallen inside me and it is dark and cold and lonely, only sadness lives there coz what adults teach is not what they do. I cannot understand why my auntie would want me to drop the case, she is a nun from the Catholic religion and she knows my uncle did evil to me, but she wants my uncle not to be punished for the evil that he has done. I want to ask her why I must be punished and live with my shame while my uncle is free, but I am too shy and I am too much crying all the time. Why won't my mother help me? Why won't anybody tell me that what I want to do is right? They only want me to do what they want so they can feel good, but it makes me feel bad. I feel that to drop the case is wrong, but nobody is helping me. Surely my mother must know I am telling the truth. She is my mother and she knows I do not tell lies, but even my mother is not helping to me. Even if I feel that what I want is right, my mind is filled with the thought that the only reason they are not helping me is that I must be wrong. My mind is being tortured by these thoughts, but I have already signed the papers so now it is too late.

When we get to the foundation my counsellor asks if I feel it is OK that I drop the case.

'No, I do not. All the time I try to do what is right, but I am not sure if I did right this time. I feel he should be punished for what he did. Now I'm not sure he will stop contacting me. I'm scared.'

All the time now I want to be alone. All day I stay in my room and pull the blanket over my head so I can stay under my shell where nobody can find me. Nobody I am talking to. My mind is filled with bad thoughts that will not go away. I want to kill my uncle. I want to shoot him for what he did and not getting punished for it. I tell the counsellor this and she says I need to rest. I need to relax because I am depressed. Every day I stay in my room till dinner. Many times I do not eat dinner. I am shy to mix with the other girls. They talk and laugh and they are happy. I used to be like that, but I am not like them now.

In my room is Merinmae and Marylyn, but I never see them. When they come in the room I pull the shell over my head and hide. I pretend I'm sleeping. Even when I'm hungry I don't eat coz I'm too shy to go to the kitchen. I feel like my rape has burned my face and left a horrible scar and I don't want any of the girls to see it. I don't want to talk. I don't want anyone to know what happen to me. During the days when I went to the Hall of Justice I ate nothing. My stomach is empty and I am always hungry, but I don't eat. Food can never fill this emptiness.

It is a rule of the foundation that you must come to the dining room and eat at dinnertime, but the housemother, ate Gailiene, is very understanding and she does not force me, even though it is against the rules. If I am hungry she says I can ask her for food anytime. Even if I don't ask her she sometimes brings a glass of milk and some biscuits to my room. She is very nice to me.

CHAPTER 3

Suicide in the Foundation

December 2009

Days are lonely here in the foundation. Every day I must stay in the house alone coz the other daughters go to school. Every day I sit in my room alone with nothing to do. There is a big mango tree in the grounds of the foundation. When I go outside I like to climb the mango tree. It makes me feel good to sit in the branches. I used to do this at home in my happy days. Sometimes I would go to the waterfall and climb the trees there. At dusk I would sit in the branches, I would look at the lights of the buildings far away in Iligan city and imagine they are the lights of Hong Kong or Singapore or Sydney. I could see the river running through Iligan and watch it flow into the ocean and I would dream that one day a boat would take me away to live an exciting life in one of those cities where the buildings reach high into the sky. These days I feel like I am not real, I feel like I have been split in two and I am an reflection of myself, that my life is happening beside me and I am only an image if what is happening.

My mind is lost inside a dark cloud and it is trapped in a nightmare that keeps twisting and turning like it is caught in some wild wind that never stops, but when my body climbs the mango tree and I curl up in its branches, the real me can see the light over the walls. It sees people in the street, they are with their children and their friends, they laugh and they have dreams like I once had. At these times my mind peaks through the dark cloud and I imagine I am a bird: that I can fly over the walls and soar aloft in clear skies. Maybe if I could fly I would wake up in some strange land and I would be young and happy again. Sometimes I try to see the tall buildings in the cities of my old dreams, but a storm surrounds them now and they are surrounded by so many dark clouds and I can barely see them. Only I see the people in the street and they are laughing and happy. I remember when I was like that, but that was another life, in this life I have no friends to talk and laugh with. The mango tree is my only friend.

Every morning at 4am the bells wake everyone for morning prayers, and every evening there are prayers at 6pm before dinner. The rule is that all daughters must be in the foundation then. On Saturday and Sunday all the daughters are here, but during the week they go to schools and colleges, only three do not.

Sailly is twenty-five. She does not go to school coz she does not know how to read or write. There is a tutor for her, the sister of Father Chang comes every day to help with her learning. Sailly is very good to me, she helps me all the time, she washes my clothes and gets me things if I need them, she is the only one I can sometimes talk to. Ate Sailly and Gracelyn do cooking every lunch time, but I stay at my room coz I am shy of the staff. And very embarrassed. I don't want them to know what happen to me.

Gracelyn is twenty-five also, she is another special girl coz also she doesn't know how to read or write and sometimes she goes a little bit crazy. Many times she acts like a child and stays in her room dressing up dolls and playing with them and talking to them like they are real. She cannot sleep at night so she is always tired. Most nights she wakes up in the middle of the night and turns on the lights so she can draw. Nobody is allowed to see what she draws, she won't show anyone, only she says she is trying to cover up the black. Sometimes she won't eat, also she has tantrums an when she does, she shouts and throws things. One day the housemother got so angry to her she threw Gracelyn on the bed.

There are many boys living in the house opposite the foundation so nobody is allowed to walk in front of their house on that side of the street, but Gracelyn did and the housemother gets much angry to her. 'Why are you breaking the rules and walking there when you know you are not allowed,' she shouts.

Gracelyn is shouting back at the housemother. 'Yes, I do that. I do that coz I like the boys and all of them is sexing me.' She is only joking at the housemother, but the housemother gets so mad she throws Gracelyn on the bed very hard. Everyone is very shocked. Gracelyn starts crying and I start crying too. I am scared. Maybe she will throw me on the bed and I am very small, if she does that to me maybe I will get hurt. The housemother is very mad, but she is mad about nothing. Gracelyn is not doing that with the boys, she is just a bit crazy sometimes.

* * * * *

On December 6th Sister Claire and Sister Claire come to visit me and they ask the housemother if they can have permission to take me for a trip. The housemother gives them permission, so they take me to Jollibee and we eat chicken, and fries and then they surprise me very much.

'We have a present for you' they say, and they give me a towel, and a wooden necklace. On it is carved hand holding a white stone. It is the most beautiful present that anyone has ever given me. Also they give me an envelope and when I open it there is a message that reads - People come and people go. Say goodbye and say hello, then get on with your life. They are both very nice, but it is very confusing with these ones coz both are Sister Claire and when I call to one to them they both answer. Now I say I will call one Sister Claire *Taba,* coz she is a very fat one, the other one I call Sister Claire *Newang,* coz she is a very skinny one. They laugh very much when I say this and I laugh too coz they are happy. I feel good when I can make people laugh and be happy. They are very nice Sisters to me.

* * * * *

Soon school is finished for the Christmas break an everyone is going on a trip to Dipitan. We are supposed to leave at midnight, but the bus doesn't arrive on time so we leave at 2am. We travel all night and when we get to the church at Dipitan we have lunch, then we go to Rizal Park to see the place where Jose' Rizal was exiled. He was a hero of the revolution against the Spanish, he is part of our culture and an important part of the history of our nation, but I never heard of him before this day.

Rizal Park is very beautiful, we stay their until 4pm taking many pictures, some of the daughters go for a swim, but no-one has a swimming costume. Swimming costumes are not allowed by the priests coz they are too revealing to our skin, we must swim in our clothes. For dinner we go to a resort and after dinner we go to Fantasyland. At Fantasyland there are lots of bright lights in some water and it shoots high in the air and keeps changing colour. There are statues of Sleepy and Dozy and Happy of the seven dwarfs and lots of little people from fairyland: there is a statue of a kung fu panda and a space woman in a funny hat and we take pictures to all of them. Eighteen rides are in Fantasyland and we ride them all. On the giant coaster I am so scared I grab ate Maricar very tight and I scream the whole way. Many times I try the Bull Fight, but always I fall off and land on my *lubot*. It hurts so much when I do this and all the daughters laugh so loud at me, but I don't mind, I laugh also coz I can make them happy. When I get off the Swinger and the Choco Tea Cup I can't keep my balance to stand up straight. I fall down both times when I get off these rides. My head is spinning so much I think I must look like my cousins when they get very drunk and fall down. I ride the Jumping Bed and the Bumper Cars and the Apollo, but on this one I get very scared. It moves like it is travelling in space and when I look out of the window the stars and the earth are very far away. This is when I get scared coz what if it never comes back again to earth. When I try the Fight Shark, the shark is always winning and it makes me so wet coz it is always spitting water on me. We ride the Galleon Ship and the Jumping Bed and the Ferris wheel. On this one many of the girls are very scared, coz it is sometimes so very high, but I am not scared. At home I am all the time climbing trees, especially the coconut trees, so being up high is not frightening for me. At 2am everyone is very tired so we go back to church and sleep in bed spacers.

All the girls are very happy and laughing on this trip. I am too, but I am still very shy and feel like I do not fit in. Ate Maricar stays with me most of the time. She is my friend coz I met her at the house of Sister Claire *taba*. She is trying to teach me how to mingle with the girls and the staff, but it is hard for me to talk to anyone, I don't know what to say. All the time there is a shadow beside me, it is watching everything I do and it gets angry if I laugh. All the time it is shouting in my mind and sometimes I feel a sharp pain like it is punching me the stomach.

* * * * *

Two times each week I have meetings with my counsellor. She wants me to tell her what happened in my past. I cannot say what happened or how I feel about this, always when she asks I am crying too much. She wants me to start a diary, but I don't want to do this, I don't want to remember all the things that happen to me that are so bad. She says it is important for her. She says I need to write everything down so she can understand what happens and how I feel, that this will help her understand so she can help me. Every meeting she says this many times, but I don't like to talk about these things or remember them. I think she can never understand how I feel. I think nobody can ever understand that there is nothing inside me now, only angry clouds, a big wind that blows the hurt around my head every night and a typhoon with rain that never stops flowing from my eyes. When she tries to make me talk or remember, I want to scream this hurt away, but I can't, I am too shy and too embarrassed to scream in front of her. I do scream. Sometimes when I can't stand it anymore I go in my room and get under my shell so nobody can see me, then I scream into my pillow so nobody can hear. I did have a diary once, but I threw it away. I don't know if I will write in a diary again.

* * * * *

At Christmas, some of the girls have vacation and they go home for two weeks, but eleven daughters are not allowed. It is too dangerous for them to go to their homes, coz the person who raped them is their father, or grandfather, or stepfather, or uncle, and they are still in their home. I don't mind to stay in the foundation, it is okay for me. I don't want to go back to my place coz the eyes of the people there judge me. Also, when I am there my cousin Ariel keeps touching me and I am scared in case he rapes me like his father and his brother Jaymark. Upper Biliran is my home, but it is a danger place for me.

Loneliness lies in my bed at night and she is cold and uncomfortable to sleep with. When my loneliness and sadness get too strong I go to the yard and climb the mango tree where I can be alone. In its arms I feel above the hurt. Beside the path to the mango tree there is a rose bush growing in a pot. The flowers are red, but the stem of one small bud is broken. When I first saw its lonely head drooping while it struggles to survive, I taped it up. Each day when I go into the yard I look to see if it has died, but each day it holds on. It is strong that little bud. I would like to pick it and take it inside to make my room happy, maybe if we shared our sadness we could be happy together, but that little bud struggles so hard that it deserves to spread its petals and grow into a beautiful flower. Roses live for only a short time, but even for a short time it deserves to look as beautiful as the other roses. I don't want it to die more quickly, so I don't pick it. I want it to live. I hope I can be like that little bud, I hope I can be strong and hold on, even though my stem is broken.

Now I am learning to mingle and I have some fun with the eleven girls who stay in the foundation, Josierose, Yana and Zelmarie are becoming my friends. One day Yana buys some fireworks and puts one in the CR and lights it. When it explodes it makes a very loud BOOM. The housemother comes running and gets very mad coz of what we do, but we do it again and again and we laugh so much because it is so much fun, but all is not fun. One night-time, all the girls in my room are tired and go to sleep early. All the lights are out, but I am not sleepy so I decide to go to the room of Josierose and Zelmarie and talk to them. Most times at night I cannot sleep. I am scared of going to sleep coz sometimes my uncle comes to my dreams, also, I don't like to sleep coz I am scared to wake up in case my uncle will be beside me again.

I do not like anyone touching me, even when we are in the kitchen or doing chores, if any girl touches me I get very frightened and want to shout and scream. Sometimes if they touch me I run to my room and put my head in the pillow and scream, but it doesn't fix me. No matter how much I scream, the afraid won't go out of my mind. I am not the same as I was when I would climb trees and stay out at night with my friends, I was never afraid then. Now I am always crying coz the scared won't get out of my mind. I cry and I don't know why, and when I cry I can't stop. At night when I cry I pull the sheet over my head so nobody can hear me, but this night, when I am going out of the room all the lights are out and it is very dark. I cannot see anything, so I never notice that one of my co-daughters is standing in front of me and she touches my arm. When she does this I scream very loud. My mind is thinking there is a spirit or a ghost in the room. I know ghosts can be there in the dark, I know them from my home.

One time when I was staying in my father's house my father ran into the room and closed the curtains very fast. He said he could see an *agta*[5] standing in the tree outside the room. My father spoke some magic words and when he looked again the agta had run away. I did not see the witch this time, only my father saw her, but in the woods near our place there are many witches. My older cousin has a farm and when I go there I always feel scared. Everyone says they have the same feeling of being scared at her place. One time when I was staying with her she put her youngest son to bed, but a cat came in the room and scratched it and made the baby's face bleed. Everybody got very scared then coz they

---

5   The Agta are actually a nomadic tribe of small negroid people living in the forested Luzon mountains. They scar their skin, let their hair grow, file their teeth into points and die them black: they wear rattan girdles and neckbands decorated with wild pig bristles. Philippine myth has transformed them into forest spirits or demons.

know that witches can use animals like cats and cows and birds and other animals to do bad things like this. When I hear my relatives talk they say witches can do many things like that. Many people in the mountains believe witches can do these things.

This night I scream when something touches me coz I think it is a witch and I don't know what the witch will do. Our housemother hears the screaming and she runs inside the room and opens the lights, but she sees nothing wrong coz already I had run to bed so she will not be mad to me. While the lights are on I peek from under the blankets and see there is no witch. After she goes back to her room I wait for a while, then I sneak outside. I feel very alone and I want to talk to Josierose, Yana and Zelmarie. Many times they are the same like me, they cannot sleep.

Gracelyn is in my room with Marylyn and Merinmae Grace, but many nights none of us can sleep coz Gracelyn turns on the light so she can draw. Never will she let us see what she draws. 'I am covering up the black.' This is all she says.

We tell the housemother we cannot sleep coz of the lights being on all the time so she makes a reshuffle of the accommodation. Gracelyn stays in the room, but Merinmae Grace and Marylyn and me move to another room.

* * * * *

I am always hungry now. After breakfast in the mornings I like to take milk and put it in a glass with some ice, then I take some biscuits and put them in the locker in my room so I can eat them later. We are not allowed junk food in the foundation, but always there are biscuits. Sometimes when the housemother is sleeping I go to the kitchen and get fruit. All the time now I am eating. When the girls are preparing meals I like to help with the cooking, even if it is not my roster. I like cooking coz I am good at it and the co-daughters like my cooking, but always I eat when I cook. I don't know why I do this, but when I feel sad or when I cry, I feel comfortable if I express myself in eating, it makes me feel better. At mealtimes I am the last one to leave the table coz I eat so much. I think maybe it is coz this time in the foundation is so boring for me. I am doing nothing all day so all the time I am always eating.

Three weeks have passed now, Christmas vacation time is over and all the girls have come back to the foundations. They share together all the things that happened on their vacation. Some are having good times and some are not, but all are happy that they could spend time bonding with their families.

* * * * *

2010

Sometimes at night I am left alone coz the girls in my room go to other rooms to sleep with their friends.

Whenever I am alone I do not sleep well. When I am alone I feel like I am in a darkness place so I curl my scared up in my shell and hide it under my blanket. I feel safe there, but even when it is hot and I am sweating my shell is a very cold and lonely place. I want to talk to someone about my scared, I want to tell someone how I feel, but I can't, I don't know how, not even to my counsellor can I explain what I feel. The words to explain what happened to me or how I feel will not come. Every word I say about this feels like the dentist is pulling out a tooth. I have had many teeth pulled out so I know what it feels like, it hurts and it leaves a hole. I was not always like this. Before my uncle did this to me I was always happy and could laugh freely. It was easy for me to mingle and make friends then, now I am too shy to express what happened or how I feel. I want to have friends, I want to laugh and have fun, but when other girls are in the room I pull the sheet over my head and hide in my shell, only when I am in my shell do I feel safe, coz nobody knows I am there.

Many mornings the girls in my room tell me that I call out loudly and shout and make moaning noises when I sleep. They say my body jerks in the bed and often I am crying when I sleep. I don't know this. When I wake up in the morning I don't know what happened in my sleep, but waking up is always a bad time for me. When I wake up I am frightened to open my eyes in case he is beside me. My mind is afraid that he is there and he will do that one to me again. Every day starts with this fear.

I am so bored, I want something to do so I talk to my counsellor and say that I want to go to school.

'Yes, of course you can go to school.' she says. 'You can go next June when the semester starts for the new school year.'

'Why? It not fare. Other girls come in the foundation and they go straight to school. They don't have to wait.'

'Yes but they are already going to school so they just transfer from their old school to the new one. You were not going to school when you came to the foundation. Your schooling was interrupted and you missed so much you have to wait till the start of the new school year.'

'But I'm so bored. I want to go now.' I say this, but she says there is nothing she can do. The rules of the foundation are that when a girl arrives, if they cannot transfer from their current school they must stay in the foundation until the beginning of the school year no matter when they arrive, this is the rule.

* * * * *I

Valentine is a day to celebrate with the heart, the love between couples and boyfriends and girlfriends, it is a day people celebrate their feelings for each other, that is why it is so special. But for me it is not only for couples and lovers. If you are single you can celebrate Valentine's Day by telling your family and friends that you love them. All the girls get together and write a Valentines card for the housemother. When we give it to her she says, 'thank you. I love you all.'

All the girls text to their family and friends and relatives to say that they love them. I text my friends at home and to Sister Claire.

* * * *

It is March. Four months I have been in the foundation with no school and nothing to do all this time. I am so bored. The co-daughters are talking about going home during their summer vacation so I talk to my counsellor about my vacation, she tells me I cannot have a vacation. The rule is that in the first year you come to the foundation you are not allowed a vacation. When she says this I get so very mad angry to her coz I have nothing in my life except boring. The black cloud that is always surrounding me gets bigger and so thick that I can hardly see or breathe. If I cannot escape from this place for eve a short while to go on vacation then my life is not worth living. I feel useless. I have no friends and no family that loves me, all the time I am scared, I am not even good enough to go to school or have a vacation. There is no use living a life like this that has nothing to look forward to, so after the meeting I go to my room and look under my bed for the razor I use for shaving my eyebrows. All the girls have razors, they keep them to shave under their arms and to make their eyebrows thin. I take the blade out of the razor and go into the CR and cut my wrist on the joint by my hand. The blood comes out red and sticky. I am surprised there is so much blood, but I don't care. I put my finger in the blood and I write on the mirror

'I HATE MYSELF SO MUCH - I WANT TO DIE.'

I watch the blood as it flows down my hand and makes a pool on the floor. When I die the other girls will have to clean it up and I don't want to bother the other girls so I get some cotton and put it over the cut so there won't be too much mess. I decide I will die in my bed so I go to my room, but ate Maricar sees some blood on the floor in the hall and she comes to my room.

'What happened to you?' she says.

'I cut my wrist.'

'Why did you do that?'

I hate myself so much and I want to die, but I don't like her to know this so I turn my face to the wall and don't answer, I am scared she will get angry. Ate Maricar takes me to her room and lays me on her bed. She puts my arm hanging outside the bed so the blood is not dripping on the sheets, then she goes to get some Butadiene and other things from ate Gailiene.

Ate Gailiene asks ate Maricar why she needs these things. I don't know what ate Maricar said coz I am in the room bleeding at that time. Ate Gailiene gives her the antiseptic and other things to put on my wrist, but the bleeding won't stop, it keeps running onto the floor and making a pool. She puts some Agua Bintida on it and it bubbles up and the blood comes frothy like red soapy bubbles that look like they are laughing at me coz

I am so useless, but in a while it settles down and stops laughing. Ate Maricar then puts a bandage on my wrist and at dinner I wear long sleeves so nobody will know what I did. For two weeks I wear long sleeves to hide the cut until it is healed, but still I hate myself and still I am not talking to anybody.

* * * * *

When it is my roster to cook I make lots of food. Each morning I mix 1 kilo of milk powder for breakfast. I make oats and Chocó milk and I am always the last one to leave the table coz I eat so much. When I cook spaghetti I make three kilos of spaghetti and eight cups of rice for twelve of us co-daughters, and they are big cups. I am getting very fat now. I am not allowed to go to school so all I do is eat coz there is nothing else to do. I am not allowed outside the compound so I stand at the gate and look through the bars. I feel trapped, like a prisoner looking through the bars of a jail and watching free people walking by and going about their daily chores. Sometimes I get so mad with boredom I punch the wall next to the gate until my hands are bleeding and getting so much sore. If ate Maricar sees me she grabs me and hugs me until I stop shaking.

Sometimes there are good times like when I climb the mango tree, then I feel like I am young again, then I even feel a little bit like I was before anything happened to me. When I climb very high in the branches I pretend I am a little squirrel that is swinging from branch to branch looking for ripe mangoes. It makes me feel a little bit free, I feel like nothing can hurt me up here. If only there was another mango tree, and another one, and another so I could climb from one to the next, and the next, and the next and keep going and I just disappeared coz nobody knows I am in the trees. Maybe then I could swing all the way out of Mindanao and make a life in another city or even another country, I could make a life like people have when they feel safe, then I would truly be free. Sometimes I wonder if I am going a little crazy.

* * * * *

Merinmae Grace is seventeen and she is crazy. My social worker told me that before she came to the foundation she was in the 'House of Hope' for crazy people. She eats nothing, only hamburgers. Her family is very poor. Today she showed me a picture of their house and it has a roof made of umbrellas. She got crazy when she was with her family coz they never had anything to eat and her uncle raped her, then a neighbour raped her. When she gets in a crazy mood she talks all the time and never stops. Often we cannot understand what she is saying. Sometimes after prayers she shouts 'Stop. We need to sing,' so all us girls stop and sing to make her happy.

* * * * *

Now it is March and school is finished for the year. Eight girls are to leave the foundation. Three are leaving coz their five years is up. The rule of the foundation is that after five years you must leave. Five girls are leaving because they are graduating from college. They are happy, the ones who are graduating. I hope one day I can be like them and have an education and be graduated, then I can get a job and look after myself.

When school finishes most of the co-daughters go on vacation, only a few of us are left here. Some daughters are not allowed to go to their place coz it is too dangerous, but I don't care what they do. I am in the foundation now for six months and still I am not talking to anyone, still when I go to my room I pull the sheets over my head so nobody can see me and they think I am sleeping. I don't want to do this. I don't want to be lonely. I want to have fun and laugh. I want to be like the other daughters, but my loneliness and my scared won't leave me. In my shell is the only time I feel safe.

* * * * *

Twice every week all the daughters have counselling sessions. My time is on Tuesday and Friday in the afternoon. Always the counsellor wants me to talk about what happened. She makes me so mad when she wants me to remember. When she asks questions about my bad times my heart beats so fast, like it is running to get away from her, but it can't because it is getting squeezed very tight in my chest, also my stomach starts to hurt and my head fills with such heavy dark clouds that my mind cannot think.

My counsellor says 'you must push away the dark clouds and remember. You must tell me what happed so I can help you.' Always she says this to me.

Is she mad!!! Does she think I don't remember? Every day I remember. Remembering is the pain that never goes away. I don't like this pain. All I want to do is hide it in the dark clouds and push it into the past so I can get away from the pain and see some happiness again, but always she is wanting me to bring my pain into the now and tell her what happened. Everything is too hurting inside to bring it into the now. If I bring it into the now it will stay with me forever and never again will I be happy, but she insists that this is what I must do. Now she makes me so mad angry with this pain that I don't care anymore. I don't care for her and I don't care to me and I don't care what happens to anyone.

At 3-o-clock in the afternoon when my session is finish I go to my room and get my razor: I go to the CR and I cut my wrist again. For a long time I stand and look at myself in the mirror. I see that I am not beautiful like some of the other girls. I am fat and I am ugly. Any beauty I had when I was young has disappeared behind the ugly in the mirror. I feel like I am two persons. The me in the mirror is in a quiet place, she is peaceful because there is no sound, no dark clouds and no pain, there is peace and there is light in the mirror. My other me wants to go into that quiet place so I can push the screaming out of my mind, but my mind is saying that the mirror is a dangerous place; blood is in there. Blood is dripping from the hand in the mirror and falling into the bucket we use to flush the CR. Blood is falling on the floor and the mirror is telling me that when there is no more blood there will be no more light. I understand that my minds are fighting, but I don't care and I don't care who wins.

When the bucket has lots of blood I throw it all over the CR and I laugh. I lean into the mirror coz I want to see if the mirror is laughing also, but the mirror is not laughing. The mirror does not care about me, it is not interested in me. I am worthless and I don't care about anybody. I don't care about my counsellor and I don't care about my life, I don't care about the girls and I don't care who has to clean up my mess. I go to my locker and wrap my hand in some clothes and go to bed. I put my hand under the pillow and go to sleep and hope I never wake up.

At 3pm the bell rings for everyone to come to the dining room to eat snacks. My blood has stop flowing now, but my sheet and pillow are glued to my wrist with the blood. Memories explode in my mind. I remember about my counsellor wanting me to talk about my bad times and my hurt comes alive again. I am surprised my hurt is still alive. I am surprised I am still alive. I don't want to be alive. I want to curl up in my shell and never wake up, but I have no choice, I must get up coz if I don't go to the dining room someone will be sent to get me. I pull the sheets off my wrist and put them in the bucket to soak. I wash and wrap my wrist and put on a shirt with long sleeves and go to the dining room. Later I will wash the blood off my clothes so nobody can see it. All the time I am eating I talk to nobody so nobody will know what I did. All the time I am thinking I am a failure. Two times I have tried to kill myself and I can't even do this properly.

* * * * *

On Sunday Father Robertson comes to visit the foundation. All the co-daughters are told we must gather in the chapel at 10am for a reflection day. Father Robertson says that for one whole day we must think about all the bad things that have happened in our lives. He says we must sit in silence and make no sound and at no time during the reflection are we allowed to talk, all reflections are private. The only sound will be some soft music he will play, but it will have no words.

We sit on the floor in a circle with all the lights turned off. There is a candle placed in front of each co-daughter and a pencil and paper. He tells us we must sit quietly and think of all the bad memories we want to get rid of out of our mind. When we think of anything we want gone, we must write it down on the paper.

In the morning for two hours we make this reflection. When I think about what happened to me, a river of sadness pours into my mind and fills me up with tears.

I feel my head getting so heavy on my shoulders that I can hardly hold it up. I cry for a long time.

My mind was full of happy once, but now all the memories of my past are sad memories. I cannot take out of my mind the things my uncles did to me or how my nun auntie won't believe me. I cannot take out of my mind how my parents and my grandparents must have known what was happening and how they ignored it. I cannot take out of my mind that my uncle punched me in front of everyone and nobody did anything to stop him or protect me, I cannot take out of my mind that my mother would not support me when I wanted to bring the case against my uncle. My head and my heart are full of the sadness of these things and the thoughts burn in my mind. They burn even more than when I fell out of the banana tree and landed in the fire. Now my hand is healed and there is only a scar to remember this, but the memories of what people id to me are blazing in my mind and I do not have scars to cover the pain. Always the memories are weeping like an open wound that won't heal. These memories are like dragons in my mind, they feel like they are in prison there and they are breathing fire. I try to put them out, but they are like devil dragons with big claws and when I try to push them away they hold on tight with their claws and they scratch and breathe fire and burn my mind.

I write down some words like Father Robertson says, but I cry more when I see the words on the paper, coz the words won't stay there. My tears fall on the paper and wash the words away so they stay in my mind. Many of the girls are crying like me. Some are making lots of sobbing noise and some are making silent crying with their tears.

At 12-o-clock we stop for lunch. During lunch we are allowed to talk, but nobody talks about their reflections, they are too sad and not nice to talk about. After lunch we go back in the chapel for more reflecting and to write down more things we want gone from our mind.

After a long time Father Robertson says to stop. He leaves the music playing very soft and makes a fire in a small pot, like a flower pot, then he says that one at a time we must all come up to the fire with the paper we wrote our words on and put it in the fire.

When I see my paper burning I do not see the words going away, I see the face of my uncle on the paper and he is burning. I think Father Robertson wants me to die the memory of my uncle in the flames, but my uncle is looking at me and he is not dying. I see his eyes and they are burning hotter than the flames. He is staring straight at me and he looks very angry. His eyes are blank, they do not see me, I think he cannot see tears or hurt or pain, these things are not in his makeup. All I see is that I am nothing to him.

When all the paper burning is finished, Father Robertson tells us he has a surprise for everyone, All the girls are excited and trying to guess what the surprise is, but he won't say. He goes to the kitchen and when he returns he brings lots of brown bags, skinny ones like big envelopes and on them is the delivery stamp 'LBC', that means, Landed with Best Care. When he says that they are letters from our families all the co-daughters are jumping up and down with happiness. Now all of us are laughing and crying again, but this time the tears are from happiness. To all of us he gives a letter.

I am so excited coz my letter will be from my mother and for nearly six months now I have not seen her or heard any words from her. I open my envelope, but when I start to read, I find it is not from my mother, it is from my nun auntie. Sadness eats me and all the happiness flows out of my stomach until my insides are empty. All the girls are opening their letters and reading, but they seem to be getting blurry and fading away. I feel like I am alone in the room. I feel like there is nothing left in this life for me, there is no family that cares for me, all I have is loneliness. Tears fill my eyes. I cry because there is no love in the world for me, but nobody knows how I feel. Nobody can see my sadness coz I look like all the other co-daughters. They are crying like me, but they are crying happy tears and happy tears and sad tears, they look the same, only on the inside are they different.

CHAPTER 4

A Third Suicide

June 2010

When school finishes, Gracelyn and Sailly leave the foundation and I get their pillows. I like my bed now coz I have three pillows. When I sleep I put one under my head, one between my knees and one I hold in my arms. If I could, I would have six pillows. Pillows make me feel safe. Now I have these pillows maybe I can sleep better.

* * * * *

Two new girls have arrived in the foundation. Their names are Nellie and Gennot. We all say hello and welcome to them. They are very quiet and don't talk much. I don't say much to them either. I know that when I arrived in the foundation I wanted to be left alone, so I leave them to have their privacy. Each new girl needs time to settle their mind in this new place before they can talk and mingle.

* * * * *

When school is about to start my social worker enrolls me at St Angela's Academy of Carmen. I am very surprised. I never expected that I would study in a private school. She enrolls me in second year high school again coz I stopped second year before I went to the foundation. Now I have something to do and this makes me happy. When I go to school I never talk to anyone except my co-daughters and my counsellor, all the boys are enemy of me. I don't trust boys and I won't talk to them so they always tease me and when they do this I shout at them. 'Leave me alone I don't want to talk you. I just want to be alone.'

One boy, Eric, he makes me so angry mad I throw a book and hit him on the face. Everybody laughs to me then. When I see them laughing I get so crazy, mad, angry that my mind leaves me and I pick up a chair and throw it at them. I miss, and they run away, but now they know what will happen if they bother me. Maybe they will leave me alone now.

Not all my classmates are bad, some are from the foundation. At school I get to know Josierose, Yana and Zelmarie much better and we have a lot of fun together. We spend all the time we can in the computer room looking at Face book. Now I am happy to be at school and to have friends.

After class, when we go back to the foundation, we have tutors to help with our studies. They are students at the Cagayan University and they come between 5pm and 6pm to tutor us every Monday, Wednesday and Friday. We are lucky coz there are lots of tutors teaching us and we get taught one to one.

After a few weeks my English teacher tells everyone that each week we need to make a poem or a story about ourselves and every Monday morning we must say a story in front of class. I cannot do this, I have nothing to share and I am too shy. I cannot talk about the things that happened to me or my feelings coz they hurt too much and when I think about them I always cry.

The teacher says everybody must do this so I try, but I never know what to say. When I get up in front of the class my body goes cold and starts shaking, and my black cloud comes back to fill up my mind with scared. I want to talk, but my heart is drumming like thunder, so loud that everybody must be able to hear it. My tongue feels so big and dry it gets stuck up in the top of my mouth and grips on there like a giant gecko that has eaten too much and is too fat to move. This happens every time I try to talk. Every Monday morning others make a speech and talk about what happened on the weekend, or about their boyfriend, or anything they like, but I am too shy and too scared. Many times I try, but never can I do this.

My teacher says we need to have a private talk about this, so after class we go to her room. She suggests that maybe we can write a poem together and I can recite the poem. She says she will help me and it does not matter if I make a mistake. She is very nice and she gives me courage. Together we write some words for me to introduce myself.

'Good morning. My name is Irene. I am 15 years old and I am from Upper Biliran ...'

Many times I tried to speak and I can't do it, but today I succeed. I talk in front of the class. I am very proud to make this talk. My teacher is very happy for me and says she is very pleased that I tried so hard. This is a good day for me.

* * * * *

Nellie cut her hair today, now it is short and sticks out all over the place. Eeeoow! She looks like a ladyboy.

* * * * *

Some nights I am in the room by myself and I can't sleep and need someone to talk to, so one night I go to the room of Shiela. We are lying on the bed talking together and after awhile she is very quiet. I think she is sleeping so I close my eyes and start to go to sleep also, but I wake up suddenly coz I feel someone touching me. It is Shiela and she in leaning over me. I think that she is trying to see if I am asleep, but no, she puts her arms around me and kisses me.

My God! I don't know what to do. She is my friend, but not like that. I don't want to make her angry, but I don't want to be kissing her and I don't want to stay there when she is kissing me, so I go back to my room.

Later I discover that she and Nellie sometimes do things together like kissing and stuff. Eeeoow! My God!

I hate boys, but I couldn't do that thing. Now I am a lesbian coz she kissed me, but I could never do that thing. Eeeoow! No way.

* * * * *

Yesterday Merinmae Grace is menstruating and she has a stain on her pants, but she doesn't know. 'You need to change your pants,' I tell her and I take her to her room to wash. When she comes out of the CR some of us co-daughters are lying on the floor and she steps over us wearing only a towel, then she says, 'can we have a fight?'

At 10pm she is still acting crazy so I go to the room of Shiela to sleep, but Merinmae Grace keeps opening the door and looking in, so I move to another bed and sleep with Sheila Mae. Then Merinmae Grace comes in the room and punches me in the back. Why did she do that? I don't know. I told the housemother and next day she transferred Merinmae Grace to room 3 with Eva Mae and Sheila. The housemother says it's not safe for me to be in the room with her.

The next day in the afternoon all the girls are sitting on the chapel floor waiting for the Priest to arrive for prayers, only the two co-daughters who are on the roster for cooking are not there. Nellie is sitting behind me and she kicks hard on my back.

'Why did you do that? I ask.

She only answer with a smile like she is having fun and beating me in some game. When I see her look at me like this I know the kick is not an accident and this makes me very mad to her, so in the kitchen after prayers, I grab her hair and I pull it very hard, then she tries to grab my hair so I punch her face. She starts crying then and runs to her room. It's not my fault she's crying, I am just defending myself coz she kicked me, but I am lucky coz the housemothers are having a meeting at that time so they are not there, only the older daughters are taking care of us so don't get into trouble for that one.

* * * * *

Sometimes there are brown outs in the foundation so now we have a job. Each Saturday and Sunday we make candles to burn if there is no electricity. We melt wax in the fryer and mix some flavour with it to make it smell nice - my favourite is orange - Then we melt a crayon to add some colour depending on what is the flavour. We mix it together and shape it in a glass mould and put a wick through it, then let it dry for one hour. After this we have siesta time from 12 till 1pm so the wax can set. The candles get collected and mostly they are taken away and sold to make money for the foundation, but some of them we keep in case of brown outs.

* * * * *

Sometimes Gayfloreen and I fight about the tasks we have to do in cleaning and tidying our room. Gayfloreen is lazy and she won't help. She doesn't understand that we need to do these tasks together and share the work. I have been put in charge of the cleaning so it is my responsibility. Every day I do my very best, but she won't help and this makes me so mad to her coz then I must clean everything by myself. When she does this I feel so lonely I sometimes get out of my mind and throw myself on the bed and scream and scream into the pillow. Now I go to the CR and see that one of my co-daughters left a blade there. I get the blade and cut myself again on the wrist. This time when the blood starts running out of my wrist I put my other hand under it to catch the blood and watch until it is making a pool in my hand. Some of the blood starts dripping through my fingers and falling to the floor. I watch it for so long that some starts going hard and al the time I am thinking of my life so long time ago.

When I was a child at my house I was always so happy, all the time I would laugh with my friends. Sometimes if we had money we would play *taxi* with one-peso coins. We would draw a square in the dirt and everyone would put a one peso coin in the square. We would draw a line at some distance away and throw another coin to see who gets closest. The person with the coin closest to the line got first turn. We would throw more coins then and the first one to land their coin in the square got all the coins. We would play volleyball and basketball and badminton and *patintiro,* Sometimes my father would cut a block of wood from the breadfruit tree and put a nail in it, then he would use a piece of glass to carve a *kasing*. He would carve grooves on the side so we could wrap a string around it to spin it in a circle. Sometimes we would spin it on our hands and it would tickle and make us laugh. Other times while it was spinning on the ground we would try to smash it with another *kasing*. There was a big rock at the back of our place at the edge of the forest. I liked to take my dolls there and play with them on the rock. Sometimes I would play house, sometimes I would pretend the rock was a big castle and my dolls were princesses and I had to dress them up and look after them. I was always playing with my friends and we'd do fun stuff like climbing the coconut and banana and mango trees. I was the only one who would climb the coconut trees to get coconuts even when I wasn't allowed coz it is so high. Three times I cut myself on the arm and leg with the *Sundang* while I was opening coconuts. The cuts bled like the cut on my wrist is bleeding now, but it's not the same, those cuts are just accidents and we would wrap them up and laugh about them. Now my childhood is fuzzy, it belongs to a faraway girl. That girl when I am a child, she is not me anymore. Now I cry all the time, I can't talk to anybody and always I feel angry. Why didn't my uncle do this to me? Why didn't he just cut my wrist and kill me so I don't have to suffer like this? Why is it me he did this raping to? Why do I pain so much and hate myself so much? These things are too much for me to understand.

While I watch the blood dripping from one hand to another and falling to the floor I ask myself these questions. I am very much not happy, but I feel like somewhere deep inside there is another me, a happy me, but this happy me is in my memory and it cannot talk and it cannot escape, she is locked behind a door in the past and cannot come into the now. Behind the door she has a cloth pushed in her mouth and she cannot move coz a big, dark cloud is holding her down and it is strong and it is heavy. I remember this other person in me when she was happy, but now all the time it is night and she is trapped in a darkness place and she is so scared Everyone is looking for her and, but nobody can see her so nobody can find her, not even me.

The blood in my hand lives in that darkness place, it is red and it is angry. I am looking at this anger when I hear a voice calling. It is saying I must go to the counselling room because the counsellor wants to talk to me. This cut is smaller than the other times, but it is bleeding and hurting very much more than the other times. I tip the blood in the toilet and put a bandage on my hand, I put on a long sleeve shirt and go to the counselling room.

One of the co-daughters saw me bleeding and told my counsellor that I cut my wrist. The counsellor is angry. 'What is happening in your mind that you would do such a thing?' Her words snap at me, she is very angry.

I stay quiet. I would like to tell her, but I don't know what to say. I don't know why I did it, only that I am very mad at Gayfloreen .

My counsellor grabs my hand and pulls up my sleeve and sees the blood on the bandage and gets more angry to me. She is tall and she leans over me. 'Why do you do this?' she shouts.

Still I keep my mouth shut. I don't know what to say. She doesn't see the scars from the first time or the second time and I cannot tell her about these. If she knew she would get even more mad to me. I don't even tell her about Gayfloreen . I don't know what to say about this, I don't know why I am so angry to her, only that she won't help to clean the room. I keep my mouth shut and I say nothing. When she sees that I won't talk, the counsellor storms out of the room in a mad crazy and leaves me alone. It's Ok that I am alone, I am always alone, but I don't know what to do so I go to my room and cry. Now I am mad to Gayfloreen and mad my counsellor also, but mostly I am mad to me because I can't even talk to explain why I cut my wrist again, I don't know why I did it.

After two weeks the cut is healed and I'm OK again, but I am still mad at Gayfloreen and I'm still mad at the counsellor and I am still very mad to myself, especially to myself. I remain very, very angry to me and I don't know why, so I eat.

I am getting very fat, my weight has gone from 36 kilos to 59 kilos and I am wearing XL T-shirt and size thirty jeans. My co-daughters say I look like a pig. I don't like them when they say this; it hurts, but I like to eat, so I don't mind too much.

* * * * *

July 31ˢᵗ 2010.

I have never experience having my own birthday party. Many times I dreamed of having a cake and balloons and blowing out the candles. I see this on TV and sometimes I go to my friend's house for their birthdays and they have a cake and candles and we burst the balloons. Often I have dreamed that one day this would happen for me and today my dream is come true. All the girls and the staff give me a card and written on the front they say

'A Simple Greetings for a Happy 17ᵗʰ Birthday'.

On the card they have drawn a beautiful lake with some plants and blue clouds. The sun is peeking over one of the clouds and it is smiling and wearing sunglasses. Each co-daughter and the staff have written a greeting on the pages and this is very nice, but the most amazing thing is that so many of them say thank you to me for being such a good friend. I am so very much surprised at this. I try all the time to make people laugh and be a good friend to everybody, but I am surprised, coz really, I think I am not such a good friend, but their words make me very happy. I have a cake and seventeen candles. The housemother says if I can blow them all out with one breath I can make a wish and it will come true, and I do it, I blow them all out with only one breath.My wish is that I can finish my studies and make a good life for myself like the words that Jenny writes for me on the card.

This is my wishes for you
More blessings to come
Healthy body
Good grades
Always be brave
Long life.

On my seventeenth birthday everybody makes me feel special and happy, I feel like a real person, like I am growing up.

CHAPTER 5

Becoming a Lesbian

Our school pageant and sports festival is coming soon and there will be a cheerleader's dance competition and many sports competitions. I am to play in the volleyball team and when we gather my group surprise me by electing me captain. Volleyball is my favourite sport so I am very honoured and happy to be captain. Now I must do my very best to help my team win. Ten players are in each team, six players and four reserves. We practice every afternoon after class and I keep very busy training with my team members. I teach them all that I learned about the game of volleyball when I played in elementary school and when I played at home. It is the favourite sport of my mother so I often played with her and my friends in Upper Biliran. Our team is training very hard and we join hands and make a pact that we will do our very best to try and win.

When the competition starts, second year plays first year, third year vs fourth year, then winners plays winners, losers plays losers, then we finish with a Championship. During the championship everybody on our team gives their best and I am very happy because our effort is worthy, we win. The counsellors and the teachers are always telling me I need to do my best, but I never really thought our team would win. Now all the teachers say they are very proud of me and I am very proud of myself. What makes me even more happy is that my crush Mary Kate is watching.

Mary Kate is in first year high school. She is younger than me, but bigger. Usually I see her in the canteen, but she is in a different class so she sits at a different table. At lunchtime I sit with Josierose, Yana and Zelmarie, but when Mary Kate is passing our table she is always looking to me. Also, our classroom is next to the laboratory and whenever she goes to the laboratory she always looks in the classroom to see where I am sitting. And another thing, every morning we have a flag ceremony and when we are in line, Mary Kate is always flirting her eyes to me. I never look back to her, I would like to but my shyness won't let me. Josierose and Mary Kate are already friends so I ask Josierose for Mary Kate's cell number. Later she introduces her to me, so after school I call to her.

'Do you remember me? I say. 'We meet with Josierose on the second floor near the library.'

'Yeah, I remember' she says. Then we talk a little bit, but not much coz I don't know what to say. Every time we see each other now I can't help smiling. I want to talk to her, but shyness hides the words from me. The first time she talked to me I can't explain what I feel, it was like little butterflies flying around and brushing their wings against my inside, it tickled and made me smile. Now we are champions in volleyball and when she congratulates me it makes me smile very wide coz I am so happy. I am thinking that I must be a lesbian now coz Shiela kissed me and now I like Mary Kate very much, especially when she is watching our win.

I was playing in the back, but we rotated and took turns at each position. One time when I was playing as a forward, Josierose took the microphone and announced to everybody, 'look at Irene, she is so inspired.' That is when I looked around and saw Mary Kate under the umbrella near the Mango tree. She had pulled her hair back into a pony tail that any pony would be proud of, it looked beautiful. The rain was falling down very hard then, but the teachers say the game must goes on rain or shine, so we keep playing.

After the game I go to the CR to change my clothes, and later, when I buy some water in the canteen, Mary Kate congratulates me. She is being very friendly and chatting, talking about exams and the pageant for Mr. and Miss Intramural and things like that, but I don't say much, I want to, but shyness sits like a rock on my tongue and won't let it move.

All my counsellors and my teachers are very proud of me. They say I did a very good job. I am so happy that we win in the championship. I am very proud of myself now and when I talk on Monday morning in school I share my happiness without my tongue being eaten by the gecko. This is the happiest moment I ever had in my life that I can share how everybody in the team tried so hard and what happened with my friends when we are playing. After I speak I am very proud, coz everybody is so happy for me.

I feel like I am getting so close to everyone now. I feel like the real me is coming back. Whenever I am with my co-daughters we are always laughing and having fun together. Many times I act like a clown to make fun for them and when they laugh I feel happy. Whenever anybody laughs with me I feel happy. I see my cousins laughing when they drink beer, but laughter is very much stronger than beer for making people happy.

Sometimes after school or on Saturday or Sunday we play scrabble or *song ka* or snakes and ladders. Sometimes ate Shane or Shiela plays the piano, then some of the co-daughters play the guitar and we have a singing time in the garage. Yana and Gennot are very good on the guitar. At night when I go to bed I like to sing, it helps me sleep. I sing love songs coz they are nice songs and easy to know the words. It is nice to have some love in my life, even if it's only from songs. We are not allowed to take the computer to our rooms so I print off the words so I know them when I sing in my bed. Whenever I sing, the girls laugh at me coz my voice is not very good for singing, but I don't care, I like to sing, it makes me happy, and it makes the other daughters laugh. Father Mark says I am gregarious. I don't know what means this word, I just know that when I talk to my co-daughters I like to act crazy or do something to make them smile, and when I am in a group everyone is always laughing. I like to be happy and I like everyone around me to be happy, especially if I am the one to make them happy.

Mary Kate and me know we have feelings for each other, so we have developed an MU, that is 'a mutual understanding', but today while I am talking and eating with Gennot in the canteen I put some food in her mouth. Mary Kate sees this and texts to say, 'I thought you don't have a girlfriend. Why do you put food in the mouth of Gennot and destroy our relationship?'

I never expected that she would get jealous like this. I am very sweet on my co-daughter Gennot, she is always obedient to the foundation rules, she is a nice girl and lots of fun, but Mary Kate does not know who Gennot is in my life. She does not know that Gennot is a co-daughter in the foundation with me. Then Mary Kate texts and asks 'Is Gennot your girlfriend?'

I explain that Gennot is my friend coz we live in the same house in the foundation, we don't have a relationship or feelings for each other, we're friends only. Mary Kate is misunderstanding what happened and I don't know what to say, I don't know how to court her coz I am too shy to express my feelings.

When I tell my counsellor about my crush for Mary Kate I think she is happy for me coz she laughs so much and so loud. I tell her that Mary Kate was watching the game and afterward I met her and we talked, but I was too shy to talk much. My counsellor laughed very loudly and so much she could hardly stop. I think maybe she likes me to have a friend. Also I share with her my worry about my studies. I am worried about my grades in mathematics and chemistry. There are a lot of problems in these subjects and I cannot understand them so I don't know how to solve them. My counsellor says I need to study hard to regain my grades because the foundation expects all the girls to have grades of 80%, but in these subjects I get only 79 and 78.

I am talking to my counsellor a lot more now about many different things, but I never tell her that sometimes I see Francis and Nellie are kissing and sleeping together and doing things. Sometimes they are together in a room in the other building when they are not supposed to be there and they lock the door. Someone told me about this so I took notice. Now I see that when there are lectures or handicraft meetings or other things we must do, Nellie is always absent because she spends her time in the room with Francis. Eeeoow! How could they do that thing? I know I am a lesbian coz Shiela kissed me and I like Mary Kate, but I could never do that thing.

* * * * *

It is Halloween and we are making decorations to put in the productivity room. We make cut-out heads from pumpkins with scary faces and some other things like ghosts and witches and spiders. We put up cobwebs made of cotton wool and a big sign at the front of the productivity room saying 'Haunted House'. All the windows we cover with foam to make the room dark and we put candles there, and when we light them they make big shadows on the wall like ghosts are trying to get free from the dark. Sherry dresses like a white lady ghost. She puts on a long white dress and covers her face with white powder so she looks like she is dead and all the blood is gone from her body. Gloryjo too, she covers herself in white powder. Nellie and Marylyn dress like black ghosts. They wear black dresses and cover their faces with charcoal, but they don't have to colour their hair coz it's already black. Josierose dresses like she has her head chopped off. Her real head is covered so you cannot see it, but in her arms she is holding another one made from cardboard so she looks like she is holding her own head. I wear shorts and use lipstick to draw lines from the side of my mouth down to my chin. I am trying to be a vampire who has eaten someone and now I am bleeding coz I drank their blood.

We make the productivity room like a restaurant and at 7pm we gather to eat food there, after dinner we have a disco. We dance and sing and laugh and pretend to scare each other and we scream, but really nobody is afraid coz we all know who is behind the costumes. There are no real wok-woks or ghosts of Halloween here tonight, only us daughters having fun. When 12-o-clock midnight comes the party finishes and everyone must take a bath coz we are all covered in powder and charcoal and lipstick and flour and other stuff. Next morning the productivity room is a big mess so after prayers we must clean it up before breakfast.

* * * * *

This summer camp we go to Balingasag Beach Resort and sleep in bed spacers in the dormitory. The owner of that resort is the president of the board of the foundation. We are divided into three groups and given the same coloured blue T-shirt to wear, then we are divided into groups and given a schedule. The first group does the cooking, the second one serves and the third washes and cleans. Five-o-clock in the morning we have exercise classes, dancing, jumping and clapping hands for one hour, then prayers, breakfast, cleaning, then we swim in the pool. Father Tong watches us in the pool. The rule is that you must wear only bra and panties coz they don't want us to get our clothes wet. We all do this, but it is very embarrassing for me. I don't like to wear only bra and panties. I am shy and I am very fat. I don't like to be undressed like this, especially in front of a priest.

After swimming there is some lectures from the counsellors. Each counsellor talks on a different subject, like good morals, dressing properly, working hard to achieve our goals and things like that. In our free time we play games like raw egg catching, message relay and longest line. To play longest line we make teams and each team must make a line by holding something that we are wearing, a towel a bracelet, socks, or anything like that. The team that makes the longest line is the winner.

We stay at the Balingasag Beach Resort four nights. On the last day we have mass in the morning then prize-giving for all the games we played. On this day there is catered food coz there is no time for cooking. This vacation is a very good time for bonding with my co-daughters and having lots of laughing fun and getting to understand them more. It's on this trip that I find out that all the co-daughters in the foundation are like me, all have being raped by someone in their family. Ate Natasha was raped by her uncle and she brought a case against him, but he was never convicted because he is a policeman. Josierose was raped by her father and her grandfather. Gloryjo was raped by her father. Jelissa and Gennot were raped by their stepfathers. Gracelyn was raped by her father. Everyone in the foundation was raped by someone in their family. When the daughters tell me these things about themselves I feel very sad, but I feel closer to them coz we are all co-daughters together in our abuse, it makes us like sisters in misfortune. It is also very bonding coz now I feel that I am not an outsider anymore,

* * * * *

My counsellor tells me that this coming semester break I am allowed to have a vacation with my family. She says I will be safe coz my uncle has run away and no-one knows where he is. If I can feel safe I am happy to see my friends again. It is a comforting feeling to know that the foundation is looking after me. Soon on my vacation I will be able to look after myself.

Christmas is coming so all the girls are busy preparing a program for the party. The foundation celebrates Christmas on December 17th. On this day there is a party and visitors come, board members, dignitaries, government officials, congressmen, sister groups of nuns, people from private companies that donate to the foundation, people like that. There is a rule for visitors to help preserve the privacy of the girls and the foundation, only two or three pictures of us co-daughters can be taken by each visitor. When they arrive they gather in the productivity room and all the daughters go there to read a program of welcome and entertain them with singing and dancing, then the visitors give us gifts. All the daughters get the same gifts, school supplies, underwear, towels, school bags, hygiene goods like tooth paste, bath soap, perfume, body lotions, shampoo etc, canned goods from Delmonte corporation to take to our families on holidays, things like that.

When gift-giving is finished everybody eats together, then there is another program of events we have prepared for them. More singing, more playing music and dancing and things like that, and after we finished, all the girls get busy cleaning coz there is a big mess in the productivity room. Soon all is back to normal again.

* * * * *

When I go on summer vacation my social worker accompanies me to Upper Biliran because I am seventeen and under eighteen years old are not allowed to travel alone, they must have someone to accompany them.

When I arrive, my mother must sign some papers to say that she received me and will take good care of me. My social worker goes back to Iligan then to pick up Divine and accompany her to Zamboanga Del Sur.

At home there is nothing to do. If I'm outside the house I'm not allowed to be alone. Wherever I go my brother follows me. My mother says that even if I go to my friend's house my brother must go too, so I spend a lot of time on my cell phone. I stay at home for some time, but my nun auntie thinks it is not safe for me so she comes to take me to her place.

My time at home is boring, but my time with her is more boring coz I can never do anything I want. With her I must spend a lot of time in the church prying for forgiveness for my sins. 'What sins?' I ask her.

'You do not pray. You do not dress properly. You wear shorts all the time. You always want to play with your friends and you do not help your parents.' This is what she says to me, but I do not understand.

'What do you mean I don't dress properly? I dress the same like all my friends. What do you mean I play with my friends? What is wrong with having fun with your friends? What do you mean I don't help my parents? My older sister does nothing. All the time they want me to clean the house and do the cooking and cleaning and they do nothing. I am a child. I do the work that is required of me, but it's not my responsibility to be a slave for my parents.' When I say this, my nun auntie shakes her head like she does not understand either. I think she is a slave also coz she is not allowed to do anything except pray to God all the time

'You must pray for forgiveness because you are not a good daughter,' she tells me. How would she know what a good daughter is? She has no children, she doesn't have any fun, only she has her prayers and God, and he does nothing to help anybody.

I do not like my first vacation, but I don't understand my feelings until I arrive at the foundation. When I get there I feel like I am leaving a dark place and arriving into sunshine and warm light. Only when I get to the foundation do I realise that at home I was always thinking I was in a darkness and dangerous place and worried about what might happen to me. Now the darkness and dangerous place is my home, always I am scared when I am there coz I never feel that I am loved or anybody cares for me. At my nun auntie's house I feel the same. I feel safe there coz nobody will hurt my body, but always my mind is being tortured. She thinks she is setting me a good example when she is praying, but when she is not praying she is always telling me I am bad. She says I never listen to my parents, but my parents never talk to me. All they say is that I must look after the animals or do the washing or the cleaning. I do these things, but they are boring. She says I am bad coz I am always fighting with them, but it's not my fault, they never make me feel like I am part of their family. I am not bad for wearing shorts or playing with my friends, our games do not cause harm to anybody. Anyway, I can't be bad, especially with my nun auntie. When I am with her I have nothing to do to be bad. I am locked up in her house all day and all she wants for me is to be like her and pray all day. I feel like none of these people love or care for me or care anything about what my dreams are or helping me to get what I want.

Is it wrong to want my father and mother and my family to love me? When I was a child I never liked to express my feelings to my family. Never could I say I feel like I don't belong to them. How can a daughter say to her parents that she feels like she is not their real daughter? My father and mother talk to my brothers and sisters all the time, they are all close to each other, they laugh and they hug each other, but they never talk to me or hug me. Sometimes I wonder if I am the real daughter of my parents. They don't make me feel like I am. My mother never even spelled my name properly when they registered it. All my family is called Lantapin, but my name is Lantapon.

When I was very young and my father was sick in the hospital in Davao and I lived with my grandparents. They looked after me then, so always at the back of my mind is the thought that maybe I came from somewhere else, that I am not the real daughter of my parents, but I don't know, I was too young to remember much about this time. I don't like my home, but I didn't realize it until I arrived back in the foundation. It feels like I am coming into the light again and it makes me wonder, when did I start to realise that Upper Biliran is a darkness place? When did I start to feel like there is only light when I am away from my home, and to feel comfortable being in the foundation?' I think maybe it started when I began opening up to my counsellor.

Until I came to know her I could not open up to my counsellor, I didn't know her so I didn't trust her. Always she hurt me coz she wanted me to remember my pain, but she was friendly. At lunchtime she would sit at our table and talk with us like she is one of the daughters. Sometimes she would join our games, and after awhile I got to like her.

Normally I have two counselling sessions each week. At first I was too shy and my memories burned my mind too much to tell her about them, but when she was around all the time we could sometimes laugh together we slowly became friendly. That is when I started to trust her and tell her what happened to me. Always she would ask the same question. 'What are your feelings about your abuse?'

'They are not good.' I tell her. This is not what I want to happen for my life. I hurt inside. I feel mad all the time and I am ashamed, coz I cannot understand why this happened to me. I blame myself and I think I must be at fault. My nun auntie believes it is my fault because my uncle told her it was my fault. She told my social worker that I am sick because my uncle sexed me and I didn't stop him. How could I stop him? He is too strong, and I couldn't tell anyone coz always he said he would kill me if I told anyone what he was doing. Then my mother wouldn't help me bring the case against him so I think she must blame me too.'

I told these things to my counsellor and we talked a lot after that. She asked me to make a list of my fears so I did. I wrote ...

> *I am afraid of seeing my uncle.*
> *I am afraid my family will find out I got pregnant.*
> *I am afraid to be alone.*
> *I am afraid my auntie will find out I am a lesbian.*
> *I am afraid to stand on my own feet and look after myself.*
> *I am afraid that I will be sent me back to my family.*
> *I am afraid to share my love to any boy.*
> *I am afraid that I will never finish my studies.*
> *I am afraid that I will never find a job.*
> *I am afraid that I can never help my family.*
> *I am afraid my health is bad coz I feel something strange I my virgina.*
> *I am afraid to have a physical check up even though I need one.*
> *I am afraid that I will fail my exams.*
> *I am afraid of being hurt.*

Sometimes we would have an activity counselling session and she would ask me to draw pictures of my family or my dreams, or sometimes pictures of places I would like to hang out with my friends. The pictures of my parents are just heads with curly hair. My parents don't have curly hair, but I am not good at drawing. When I look at them now I see that only my father is smiling. I like my father sometimes. Even if he never gives attention to me he does take care of me and accepts what happened in my past. I would like to draw a picture of my grandmother on my mother's side, coz she is the only one that would sometimes hold me. I would like to draw her smell coz when she held me close and her smell filled my nose, I felt safe, but I don't know how to draw a smell. When I draw the picture of my favourite nook where I would like to hang out with my friends I draw the place where I sit at school. In the drawing there are three tables and each has two bench seats and two chairs and they sit under a big Nara tree. Wild flowers grow between the seats and behind them is a grove of three more Nara trees. In my mind the flowers are yellow, but in the picture they have no colour coz the pictures are drawn with a writing pencil. I would like to have drawn the smell of roses that comes from the Nara tree, but I don't know how to draw this smell either. My favourite nook has clean air and is somewhere far away from everyone, but where I can still see them. In the drawing all the seats and tables are empty; there are no people in this drawing.. I don't know what my counsellor thinks of these drawings, they are pretty bad.

Until I talked to her I thought I am to blame for what happen, coz all the people at home are dark-side people and they judge me, they think it is my fault and they blame me for what happened. I am just thirteen years of age when my bastard uncle raped me, but they say what happened is my fault. How can it be my fault? Sometimes I feel guilty. I am never sure if it is not my fault. Sometimes I feel like it is, but I don't know why. I think that maybe I did something to make him rape me, but I don't know what.

When I told my counsellor all these things, I thought she would say I am bad, but she did not judge me. She says what happened is not my fault. Maybe I believe her. I think maybe she is right.

When I arrived back in the foundation after my vacation all the daughters are talking and sharing their happy and sad experiences. During the vacation Josierose's stepfather touched her while she was sleeping and she woke up very scared. Her real father is in jail in Davao coz he raped her. Her grandfather raped her also, but he is dead now. Divina had problems this vacation. Her neighbour and her mother are sexing each other and when Divina found out she got very angry with her mother, so they were fighting all vacation. Next day we are back to normal again following the policy and rules in the foundation.

* * * * *

Father Mark announces that we are going to take a food trip to the Mga Bata Foundation for abnormal people. He tells us to our locker and find some special gift we can give to the people there. I get a towel and

the necklace Sister Claire gave me when she took me
to Jollibee coz this is the most special thing I have.
Also I get my favourite T-shirt with the word 'Boracay'
written on the front. I received this at our gift giving
last Christmas and it is my favourite shirt coz one
day it is my dream to experience playing on the white
sand of Boracay and swimming in the water there. On
television they say that Boracay has the clearest water
in the Philippines, and when I see posters of it the water
looks so clear you can see through it like a window.

Us co-daughters cook spaghetti and fried chicken
and rice and pack juice to take to the abnormals.

In the Mga Bata Foundation there are five adults,
they are old woman, but they have the minds of babies
so they are not able to look after themselves. It is a
very big foundation with a big playground where all
the children can play games. There are many children,
all are aged over five years and have been abandoned
by their parents. Oh My God! When I see them! OMG!
I cry so much.

All the co-daughters are given one child to look
after for the day. One daughter is given a child who
was born premature so he is not formed properly. His
tongue is stuck to the top of his mouth and he cannot
talk. Another daughter is given a child who has no legs,
only metal for legs. Most have *sipon* running from their
noses and many have saliva bubbling from the side of
their mouths. Some of their heads falls to the side and
their eyes roll around like they are balls in a pinball

machine. The child I am given is very skinny and he has no eyes. They tell me he was aborted by his mother and left abandoned in the rubbish. When someone found him his eyes was eaten by insects and decayed. Now he will never see coz he has no eyes, all he has is holes, but no eyes.

I play with my boy, but sometimes I am blind like him, I cannot see because all day my eyes are full of tears, I cannot stop them. I care for this boy. I feed him and play with him and we laugh, but in me heart I feel his pain and hurt so deeply. I give to him the necklace that Sister Claire gave me, but when I do this I am sad because the necklace is very beautiful, but he will never know that. All the time I am there I am so sad for these kids, but one child makes me very happy. He is about nine years old and when we are leaving he says, 'Thank you so much for coming and helping us.'

I cannot stop my tears from flowing when he says this. Their life is so sad, but he is happy, and he has made me happy that, even if it is only a short time in one day, we can do something nice to make their lives better.

When we return to the college the counsellor says we must write a reflection paper about this visit. When I write my reflection I cannot help crying again. I cry coz I feel so lucky that I am complete and normal, then I cry coz every one of us co-daughters is perfect, even if we have experience the worst, still we are complete and we have families, even if some of them are bad we have never suffered being abandoned like these children. I feel very sad for the children coz even if we make them laugh and help to feed them, they cannot survive like us. I think all we can do is to make their lives happy for a short time. It is good that father Mark got us to do something to help, and I realise that I do not own all the problems in the world. I smile at my good fortune, but I am sad also, I understand how much their mind is tortured by the feel they have inside. I believe they must feel like their lives are hopeless and I know what it is like to feel hopeless.

* * * * *

Indayjo is a nice girl, she is very young, every time we are together we talk and laugh a lot coz she is so friendly. We have become like sisters. When she came to the foundation she didn't know how to eat with a fork and spoon. At home she ate with her fingers like my family do. I learned to eat with a spoon and fork at Auntie Nona's house in Aurora, but at home we never have these, we eat with our fingers.

Indayjo. came to the foundation coz her father raped her for a long time like my uncle did to me. Each time after he finished he would make her sit on the bed and he would throw knives in the wall by her head. He told her that if she told anyone what he did he would throw a knife in her heart. She was like me, she was so scared she didn't tell anyone for a long time, but eventually she told her teacher and it was reported to the police. She brought a case against him, but her father and mother ran away and now she doesn't know here they are. Now she has no family.

At first she never talked to anyone for a long time. Most new daughters are like this, they don't talk much for about one month, but me and Indayjo took longer than this. Now we are good friends. I gave her one of my T-shirts and she wears it under her school uniform. We are always laughing and singing together coz she can play the guitar. I try to play the guitar also, but I am not good at this. I am not good at singing either, but I don't mind. I sing coz it makes the other girls laugh and that makes me happy.

* * * * *

My room is room three in the first building and my bed is near the window. It is hot in the foundation so when I sleep I keep the window open and put my hand outside to try and stay cool. One night when I was in the computer room I need some notes, so I went to my room to get my notebook, but while I was there I saw someone racing very fast passed the window. At first I thought it must be one of my co-daughters going to the visitor's CR, but she was going so fast I cannot know if it is a boy, or girl, or what, so I ran outside to see. I slammed the door of my room and the door of the kitchen so they will know someone is there and not get frightened, but no-one is in the CR. When I return I think that I look scared, coz the housemother asks what happened.

'I saw someone passing the window going very fast to the CR, but when I went to look, no-one was there.' I tell her this and when they hear me all the girls get scared. Some are thinking it is a person and some are thinking it is a ghost, but they are only guessing, nobody knows. After that my housemother tells me I must always close the window at night, but the window is like a mirror, at night you cannot see out, all you can see is your reflection. When I close the window I feel that if someone is outside, they can see inside and they might be watching us.

Gayfloreen says she is not scared of ghosts. She says it is a good thing I went to the visitors CR, coz in her religion, when a person walks in the footsteps of a ghost, they believe it will chase away the ghost and it can do no evil. Gayfloreen comes from a very faraway place on Dinagat Island. Her uncle is like a god on that island. They have a religion there called *Gaba* and the gods in this religion are people, so he is a person-god. Gayfloreen says many young girls come and offer their virginity to him and he sexes many girls, but he raped Gayfloreen when she was only eight years old and this is why she has come to the foundation, for protection from her uncle-god.

Most of us girls never talk about what happened in our past. When new girls come to the foundation they are mostly very shy and don't talk very much for the first month. After one month sometimes we talk a little bit and ask what happened, but none of us like to remember these things. When my counsellor asks me to write things down and I think of things in my past, it makes me dream and I wake up scared and crying. On these nights I can never go back to sleep coz my mind screams with so much noise. When I try to escape into the silence, my sleep is never quiet, too many memories shout in my mind and keep me awake.

I don't know if I dream very often, but maybe I dream a lot, coz sometimes the daughters in my room say I cry and call out in my sleep. When I wake up I don't remember my nightmares, but I think I have many coz sometimes I wake up very sudden, like I've had a shock and my sheet it is wet from sweating. Sometimes I feel cold and can't stop shaking, I don't know why. When this happens it makes me feel very alone. My mind cries out for somebody to help me, but there is nobody. I want someone to hold me in their arms and make me feel safe, but I don't want anybody to touch me. I want someone to stroke my head and to smell the safe smell of my grandmother like when I was a child, but this can never happen now, I don't trust anybody to be close like that. Even when other co-daughters are in the room I feel lonely. I don't know why I have these feelings. I am not intelligent you know. My mind cannot understand why loneliness haunts me so much and makes me sweat when I am cold.

I am not the only one who talks in my sleep, all the girls do. Sometimes I hear Gloryjo talking in her sleep and she even talks in English.

Not all is bad though, one time when I have a fever, the housemother gave me some medicine, but after I took it I still do not feel well, my body was sweating, but I felt very cold, so went to bed and covered myself with a sheet. Still I couldn't get warm. I borrowed the sheets of Sherry and Mareanna who were in the room with me. They are laughing and having fun at my expense, joking at me for being sick. I am laughing with them also, but while we are laughing my right arm starts going stiff. I cannot move it and when I try to get up my right leg won't move either.

'Can you help me please? I can't move my arm or my leg.' I say. They laugh more then, coz they think I am joking, but I'm not. I'm struggling to open my hand, but I can't. Then I start to get scared. When they see this, Sherry tries to pull the sheet off me, but my hand is all twisted and will not let go. Now they know it's true and something really is wrong. Sherry goes to tell the housemother, but while she is gone Mareanna massages my hand and the feeling starts coming back. By the time the housemother arrives I am already well and can move my hand and leg and I'm okay.

* * * * *

The next time we had another room shuffle I was moved to the third building, but there are strange noises around this room. Sometimes there are footsteps in the hallway in the middle of the night and sometimes when everyone is sleeping the shower starts running. It is my job to lock the main door of the building from the inside. I do this every night, so I know it cannot be the housemother, she can't get in. I tell my counsellor what I hear and she tells me that when the priests bought the property and made it a foundation, everything got renovated, but before that, this building was a big private house. The owner built it around a giant mango tree. It was cut down when the priests made the renovations, but before that someone committed suicide in the bathroom of the old house.

When she says this I think that what I must be hearing is the spirit of that person who made a suicide there. Then she tells me that on one occasion, when all the staff were meeting in the room next to the productively room, they heard someone flushing the toilet. One of the staff went to check who is there, but it was empty. They thought this is very strange so they left the door open, but during the meeting the door closed by itself. All the staff saw what happened and they got very scared, so they stopped the meeting and left the room.

* * * * *

Sister Claire *taba* and Sister Claire *Newang* are graduating from College and they ask permission for me to attend their graduation. I never expect the housemother and the board to allow me to go, but they do, and at the graduation I meet Father Vegas. He is very fat, American I think. His accent is funny, not like I hear on American movies so I'm not sure if he is American. When we meet he hugs and kisses me.

Wow! I get so scared then. I never expect that a priest would kiss me in my face. This is the first time ever something like this happens to me. Because it is such a special occasion, Father Vegas wants to wish The two Sister Claire's well and great success in life, so after the graduation he takes us to a restaurant for dinner. The co-daughters say he sometimes makes treats like this. They say Father Vegas is very kind.

* * * * *

One day there is no water in the foundation, I don't know why. All the co-daughters have to carry buckets to a neighbour's house to fetch water for our bath and to flush the CR. I walk with Princess and while we are walking she opens up and starts to talk to me. She came to the foundation awhile ago, but this is the first time she has really spoken to anyone. She tells me she was raped by her father and is bringing a case to him so she cannot stay at home anymore. She is like me, she is like many of us daughters, we are all afraid of what will happen to us in the future when our five years are up and we have nowhere to go that is safe. We are chatting as we walk, but after we get back to the foundation and carry the water upstairs, I decide to have fun and slide down the handrail, but halfway down my foot gets caught and I tumble head over heels and land on my *ekog*. It hurts very much. Princess and the housemother look very shocked, but I am laughing and rubbing my *ekog* so they laugh with me. Then all the co-daughters come to find out what is happening and everybody is laughing at me. I don't mind, I like to make them laugh. I like it when people are laughing and happy, even when it is because I hurt my *ekog*.

* * * * *

July 31st 2011

On the last Saturday of each month there is a celebration for all the co-daughters who have a birthday during that month. There is a big party with spaghetti, salad, rice and BBQ and we sing karaoke and have fun. Sherry and my birthday are in the same month and we are the same age. Sherry' birthday is on July 6th, my birthday on 31st so in 2011 we both turn eighteen and celebrate our birthdays together.

The counsellor tells me to wear a cocktail dress. 'Eighteen is a special coming of age birthday and you should dress nicely for the party,' she says. Sherry does, but I refuse. I am too shy to wear a dress. I don't like dresses, I am too big and boyish. I wear a T-shirt and long shorts like a boy.

My eighteenth birthday is a very special day in my life. I am given eighteen roses, there is picture taking and my co-daughters do some singing and dancing that they have prepared especially for Sherry and me. We each have a big cake covered with blue icing and eighteen candles so we can blow out our own candles. When I blow out the candles I make a wish under my breath that sometime in my future, life will be good to me. When we cut the cakes, we put our fingers in the icing and splash it on each other's face, then, all the co-daughters do the same to each other and even on the face of the counsellors. Everybody is laughing and nobody minds, even the counsellors are joining in the laughter and enjoying themselves with us.

The party finishes at twelve midnight, then the girls must go to wash the dishes, but it is my birthday so I don't do this. Sherry and I just relax and watch TV for awhile. This is our coming of age birthday so now I am an adult. I don't really know what I am coming of age to do, but it feels good to be an adult. Now I can do things I am not allowed to do before. I don't know what I can do, but even if I don't know, this is the best ever day of my life.

Next day is Sunday, and Sunday is always a bad day for me. For three hours each Sunday we have time when outsiders can visit the daughters. Normally it is the families who come to visit, but my family never comes, I am left alone. Even on my eighteenth birthday nobody comes, only my nun auntie comes occasionally and sometimes Sister Claire.

* * * * *

December 2011

At the Christmas party this year, after we had performed the pageant for the guests we are sitting in the productivity room waiting for Father Mark to finish making a speech so we can have the present giving. The women guests are all sitting with their legs crossed and the men are sitting with their knees apart. I am sitting next to Josierose and I nudge her with my elbow, 'look.'

She follows my eyes and sees one visitor with a big bulge in his pants. We can't help it, Josierose and me are laughing and everyone is looking at us, but we can't stop, and no one even knows why we are laughing.

In gift giving this year all the girls get a teddy bear. Mine is yellow with a red jacket, he is called Winnie the Poo. I love Winnie, he is my friend. When I go to bed at night and I feel lonely I hold him tight and he makes me feel safe.

CHAPTER 6

Father, Oh dear! Father

March 2012

School year is ending soon so the teachers have organised a class bonding to say goodbye. At lunchtime all the students gather in the shade of the big Nara tree at the side of the soccer field. Teachers from all the different levels come and everyone brings food to share. One of the teachers brings a big cake and one of the boys takes some of the cream from the cake and smears it on face of one of the girls. Then everyone does the same thing until we all look like laughing cream cakes. We do this at all the parties when we have big cakes with lots of cream.

We are going on vacation soon so everybody is very happy. This is a very good bonding time for us classmates and we are all happy, but I am also sad. My counsellor tells me that when we come back from vacation, all co-daughters will change to a different school. My counsellor says that I must say nothing to any of the co-daughters or my school friends, coz this has not yet been revealed to everyone.

* * * * *

This year ate Maricar, ate Kathy, and ate Denz graduate from college. After the graduation program, ate Natasha and Josierose and me are to ride in Father Mark's car back to the foundation where there will be another graduation celebration and a birthday party. While we are waiting I sit in the front seat beside Father Mark. Ate Natasha, Josierose and me are making jokes about bad girls, but we don't want Father Mark to hear what we are saying, so I am leaning over the back of the seat and we are whispering. We are waiting for Father Mark's friend Renella. Father Mark invited her to join the party, but Josierose and I don't want Renella to be there, she is our school friend and she is nice, but it is embarrassing for us coz she doesn't knows what happened to us co-daughters or why we are in the foundation. Father Mark hears us laughing about bad girls and gets upset. 'Be quiet, you are a bad girl too,' he says, but he doesn't say this to all of us, he says it directly to me coz I am so loud and the one laughing so much. His words shock me very much. He is wrong. I am not a bad girl. I never do bad things to anybody. It's not my fault my uncle raped me. My bastard uncle did bad things to me and now Father Mark thinks I am a bad girl and it's my fault I'm in the foundation. His words make my head spin. One minute I am having fun with my friends and the next the put a black cloud in my head and puts me in a bad mood. My day is destroyed and I start to cry. I storm out of the car and get in the back seat coz I don't want to sit next to him anymore. When Renella arrives, she sits beside Father Mark. All the way back to the foundation I cry, and when we arrive I go directly to my room. I am not anymore in the mood to join in the celebrations.

Awhile later Father Mark comes to my room. He tells me the mass is starting, but I am hiding under my shell and ignore him. Soon after that my counsellor comes into the room and asks what happened. 'Father Mark told me I am a bad girl. I am not a bad girl. I was just having some fun laughing and joking. It's not my Fault I am here. I am not bad.' I tell her that Father Mark's words upset me very much and made me cry.

My counsellor says I need to join the program, but I tell her 'No! I am not a bad girl and I don't want to see Father Mark.' My voice is very definite and when she hears this my counsellor leaves the room. I think maybe she goes and talks to Father Mark coz after mass he comes back. He asks if he can apologise for what he said that made me feel so bad. I refuse to look at him, while he talks I face the wall and don't turn around, even one word I won't say to him. He hurt me very much and I won't accept his apology. When I sense that he is not there I look around and he is gone.

Later my counsellor comes back and tells me I need to eat, but I refuse. I let her think I won't eat because I am still mad to Father Mark. I am mad to him, and I am hungry, but the real reason is that I have a very big pain in my stomach, but I don't tell her this. I want her to believe that I am still mad with Father Mark.

Indayjo brings some food to my room later, but I don't leave the room. After the program all the daughters clean the dishes and tidy the productivity room, and while they do that our housemother comes to ask what happened. I listen to her, but I never answer, even to defend myself. She can think what she likes. I am not a bad girl. I do not do bad things. I am very upset and not in the mood to talk to anyone so she never hears that I was just laughing and having fun and Father Mark got upset at me for no reason.

Next day my stomach is still very sore. I tell my social worker and she tells my counsellor and they take me to the hospital. The nurse gives me something to drink and they make some tests, then the doctor says that my ulcer has attacked me again. They make me drink some more medicine and give say I must drink this medicine and take the tablets three times every day until the pain stops.

* * * * *

When we go on vacation the staff say that all girls eighteen years and above can travel alone. I am very proud that I am an adult now and can travel alone. When I get home I find that my grandfather on the side of my mother is very sick. Something is wrong with his throat and he cannot eat. His body has shrunk so much he looks too small for his skin. He is old and now he is so bowed in the middle that he looks like he has barely enough strength to hold up his head. I think he will die soon.

I stay with my mother, but our house is very small so I must sleep on the same sleeping mat with my brother Jerome and my elder sister, but every time one of them moves I jump coz I think my uncle is there. When Jerome moves I want to scream and run away. I know he is my brother and he is a good brother, but some of the co-daughters were raped by their brother so I am very scared now of all boys and men. Even when I walk in the street and some boy says hello I never look at him or answer him. I am so scared of men.

After summer vacation we return to the foundation on June 23rd. On Sunday night the housemother says we must gather in the *sala* for an announcement. Father Mark tells us that the board and staff have made a decision that all the daughters studying in St Mary's Academy of Carmen will transfer to the Blessed Mother College in Iponan. He says the counsellors and the social workers have already enrolled us and we start the next day.

Our new school is not nice. The school is like a public school. It is an RVM school run by the Religion of Virgin Mary nuns. I have ten classmates, Josierose, Yana, Zelmarie, Marilyn, Gloryjo, Sarah, Jude, Jerryvan and Pablo. I decide I will do my best not to fail any of the subjects and as days pass I learn to love our school and accept what it looks like.

After some months in the new school the teachers in English, Biology and Mathematics have become very close to us, but the teacher in economics gets mad at our English teacher, I don't know why, so the Principal changes all the classroom teachers and the principal becomes our economics teacher. Now every time she enters the classroom she is angry at us, but nobody knows why. Teacher Amy teaches mathematics and chemistry and she is very good. She explains everything slowly and clearly and if we have a problem understanding she reviews for us until we understand. She helps everybody very much.

In fourth year HS we co-daughters have no tutors and the foundation rule is that you must get a minimum of mark of 80 in all subjects, but my mathematic grade is only 79 and below 75 you must repeat. I am worried now so I apply myself much more to my studies. Everywhere I go I take my books to study and there are so many and they are all heavy.

Marianne is the only girl in our new school who knows what happened to us girls from the foundation. Sometimes the co-daughters have to go to court for a hearing for the cases they are bringing against their abuser so they are absent from school. When this happens some girls ask why we are absent. We don't say, just that we have something to do, but Marianne is all the time asking why we are in the foundation and why some girls are absent. She is a good friend, so I tell her. She was a good friend before I told her, then after I tell her she becomes a very good friend to me. If I need anything she gives it to me. She gives me food if I am hungry, or crayons, or pencils, anything I need. She is a very, very nice girl Marianne.

* * * * *

There is another foundation for abandoned babies in Cagayan de Oro and all the co-daughters are told to get ready for a visit there. When we arrive we are told that all the children are under five years old. In one room there are twenty-five babies in cribs. They are very small and all are crying coz there is only one housemother to feed and look after them. Two were newly born in the last two days. We are not allowed inside this room, we can only look at them through the glass. I feel so mad at the mothers of these babies. Why do they have babies if they don't want them? Why do they have sex if they cannot look after their babies?

We play games with the older children and try to make them laugh, but two boys cannot walk straight coz all their legs and hands are twisted. My counsellor says they have Cerebral Palsy. It makes some of their muscles all twisted and stiff so they cannot move them coz their brains and nerves cannot work properly. One boy has his eyes crossed in the middle so they are always looking at his nose, but some of these kids are good and healthy and we have lots of fun playing games with them. We bring food for the children. I make spaghetti Philippine style. I use tomato sauce, ground pork, hot dogs, condensed milk, nestle' cream and cheese, it is very sweet. I like it like this and the children do too.

* * * * *

Every Saturday night at 9pm in the productivity room we watch *'Maalaala Mo Kaya'*, it is a program that tells true stories about people in the Philippines. Many times they have stories about girls like us, but every time it's about rape, my eyes get red and my tears fall down and wet my face, I cannot stop them. When I see girls suffering like us, I think the men in my country must be very bad. So many times us girls are raped and always it is a relative or their father or grandfather who is doing it. I am so scared of men now, especially men who are my relatives.

Before we watch *'Maalaala Mo Kaya'*, the housemother puts on a movie. We are never allowed to watch movies that have kissing or loving, the movies are always about success and people overcoming their problems. This night the movie is a comedy about some boys and girls in hospital. The doctors are all making mistakes in their operations, taking the wrong pieces out of the wrong people then trying to put them back, but they always put the wrong pieces back in the wrong people. The doctors are so silly coz they cannot decide who should have what operation. This is a very funny show and everyone is laughing so much. I am jumping up and down and laughing and rolling on the floor so much I nearly pee my pants coz it is so funny. Then one of the boy's father comes in and gets very mad at the doctors and I stop laughing. Suddenly tears flow to my eyes and I start crying and I can't stop. All the daughters are looking at me and asking what is the matter, but I just shake my head. I can't speak to tell them. I am quiet now. Through the tears my eyes are watching the TV, but my mind is thinking of my parents and my family.

My mind is wishing I had a good father who cares for me. My father is a good man, he works hard when he can get work, he never drinks or smokes, but he is very strange. Whenever we have visitors, whenever relatives or friends come, he never says hello to them, he just goes to his room and stays there. But what is the worst for me is when he gets crazy angry and beats us. One day he got a stick and beat my brother so much my brother was getting weak and falling down, and still he didn't stop until my mother grabbed him and held him so tight so he cannot move his arms to hit my brother anymore. He hits me too. Sometimes it is my job to look after the animals. I like looking after the animals, especially the pigs, coz one time our mother pig has fifteen piglets and I helped deliver them and clean their faces after they were born. My father gave one to me and every morning I would feed it milk from a bottle so it would grow big and strong, but sometime when I forget, or I am too tired to look after the animals, then he gets a bamboo stick and beats me on the *ekog* and it hurts very much. He beats me till I go out to look after the animals and he chases me and beats me so much I can't even sit down coz my *ekog* is so hurting. One time I had a fight with my sister coz she was wearing my shorts and my father beat me across the back with the rope he uses for the animals. The first time he did that I promised that one day I would run away from this place and never come back. My father is good man sometimes, but I cry, coz on the TV the boy's father is acting so caring for him and trying so hard to look after him. The boy's father blames the doctors, coz it is their fault, not the boys fault. This is when my mind remembers that my father never cares for me and never protected me when I needed it. I wish I had a good father who looked after me and protected me. I cry, but I cannot tell my co-daughters why, I am too embarrassed.

* * * * *

When Father Vegas comes to visit he makes everyone happy, so we try to make him happy too. When he arrives we stand in line with a letter pinned on our backs and when the housemother says 'go,' we turn around and it reads, 'Welcome Father Vegas.' I am happy that this makes him happy, but I cry also coz when father Vegas visits we have to wear a skirt. I don't like to wear a skirt. I have big calves and my legs are not nice, I get shy if people see them. I am not feminine you know, I am fat now and I am not beautiful. I am insecure about my shoulders coz they are wide like a boy and this makes me shy to wear a string top. When I lived at home I was a tomboy. Josierose and ate Natasha and Yana, say I look like a ladyboy. The first time they said this I was so disappointed to them. I accepted their words, I laughed loudly and acted like they are joking and I didn't mind, but even if it's true, I felt hurt.

* * * * *

My grades are improving now. I have been studying very hard and I got 82 in Chemistry and 85 in mathematics. Now I am happy with my grades.

* * * * *

Everybody is excited because the Christmas party is coming and soon we will go on vacation. All the classes at school are busy making Christmas trees. Our class makes a bamboo frame and on it we put strips of yellow plastic going from the top to the ground. On the top there is a star made from yellow water-cellophane. We make ribbons from red and yellow string and put circles with cellophane all around the tree. We try to make our tree beautiful, and as attractive as we can coz there is a prize for the class with the best tree. We think it looks very beautiful and we are hoping it will be worthy of a prize. Now everyone is excited waiting for the teachers to give the result of the judging.

CHAPTER 7

Typhoon Sendong

December 2011

Our Christmas party in the foundation is December 17th. In the productivity room we put up a Christmas tree and a big sign with the words, 'The best of all gifts around a Christmas tree is the presence of a happy family all wrapped in each other's arms.' The co-daughters are very happy to have each other, together we are the BDF family. Today is Thursday December 15th. At night we are practicing our dance for the presentation the day after tomorrow, but it is raining very hard and the wind is blowing the rain against the windows and making lots of noise. During practice there is a brown out. When the lights go out I scream. I grab hold of the girl closest to me and hold on tightly. I don't know even who I am holding onto until some of the girls light candles and we can see again.

Sometimes we have brown outs in the foundation and they scare me very much. Many times my uncle would come to my room at night when it is dark. I would wake up and he would be beside me and when he saw I was awake he would put his hand over my mouth and hold me down and rape me. Darkness is a very scary place for me.

Outside the windows it is dark as far as we can see. The lights have gone out everywhere in the entire barangay, but we don't stop practicing. When the candles are lit we dance in the candlelight until it is time to go to bed.

The bell rings at 4am to wake us for morning prayers, but while we are praying we hear a neighbour shouting that a flood is coming to our subdivision. Everybody gets in a panic when we hear this coz we don't know what to do. All of us run to the first building where the housemother and Administration Officer get us organised. 'Take all the equipment and put it upstairs in the third building where it will be safe,' they say.

We pick up the important things like the TV, sound system, fan, school supplies and things like that, and we carry them to the higher rooms in the third building so they will not get washed by the flood. At 6am a group of us daughters are sitting upstairs in the third building. Dawn has broken and when I look out the window I see that the rain has stopped. The sky is clear and the sun is already shining brightly. We start to relax coz it looks like it will be a nice day.

'It looks like the flood will not come' I say, but as these very words are leaving my mouth I hear Givina shouting and she sounds scared. I run to the first house. The flood and I get there at the same time. The water is running under the gates and coming toward the kitchen. I am so shocked I don't know what to do. One of the co-daughters shouts at me to carry a sack of rice upstairs to the third building. Normally I cannot lift a sack like this on my own, but now I am in such a panic I don't feel the weight and carry it upstairs by myself. When I return, the water is all around the house. The flood is now coming so fast that the water in the kitchen is already up to my ankles. Sherry, Marianne and Ailine are still inside the second house and can't get out coz the flood is so strong they cannot open the door. I help them climb through the window and for a minute we stand waste deep in water wondering what to do.

Sherry, Marianne and Ailine start to cry. The flood is coming very fast and everyone is very scared. There is lots of danger, but for me the feeling is not of danger. It is as though I am in another place watching myself in the water. I hear shouting, a dog is barking somewhere in the distance, but there is no sound of cars or jeepneys or motorbikes or tricycles, the normal buzz of engines and the blaring of horns is gone. There is no wind or rain, all the noises of a normal day have gone and left a silence more quiet than the hills of Upper Biliran. For a moment I stop to feel the silence. The danger seems surreal, like everything is happening in a pleasant dream. The sun is shining and the day seems bright and peaceful. The water is rising around me, but it is creeping silently and making less sound than the water when I flush the toilet. There are birds in the trees, my friend the mango tree is nursing a squirrel with a white bushy tail. It feels like I am an actress in a movie and across the screen everything is moving in slow motion, there is danger, but somehow I know it will not hurt me. The world this morning is so peaceful and quiet I cannot be afraid, but in my mind I know I should be. I know that when everything seems quiet and peaceful that is when danger sneaks up and rapes you.

'Where is BD?' Sherry asks.

BD is our dog; she is named for the *Bitoon Sa Langit* Daughters. BD is a girl dog coz no boys are allowed in the foundation, not even boy dogs. She lives in a small house in the yard and must be tied up all the time coz when she is loose she eats our shoes, and when she goes into the *sala* she makes so much noise standing in front of the mirror and barking at the dog in there. If she gets out of the yard she goes crazy and runs away, then all the daughters have to form teams to go find her.

We get BD from her small house, but she is very frightened and tries to pull away. Nobody can get away though, not even us, coz now the water is rushing under the gate like a torrent and pushing on the other side of the gate so strongly, we cannot open it to get into the street. When we all push together the gate opens a bit and the water comes rushing in so fat I get knocked down in the rush and washed toward the door. Together we run into the street to join the other girls, but we don't know what to do so we just stand together and wait. Now that the gate is open we watch water pouring into the compound. It rises so fast it soon creeps up toward the roof of the first building and the second floor of the third building, but we are safe in the street coz the street is higher than the foundation. Where we are standing it is only up to our ankles and up the road we can still see the street.

Most of the girls are very scared. Gennot is so scared her hand is frozen and she cannot move. A neighbour, a very big man, he puts Gennot on his shoulders and carries her until we find the housemother and the counsellors and together with many people who live in the area we start walking to Guisano Mall. People say the radio told them to go there coz it is on higher ground and they will be safe there.

Many people are crying. One lady is caught in deep water and being washed away toward the ocean. She is holding on to a big plastic water bottle and splashing, trying to get to the road where she can stand up. Some people pull her to safety and she is okay. People are carrying TVs, or boxes of clothes or other things. Many carry babies, some look newly born. Some old people with grey hair and bent bodies are struggle on wobbly legs like my grandparents. One lady is screaming coz her baby is washed away in the flood and she cannot find it. Two people are carrying the bodies of people who are dead. Many people are crying coz they cannot find their families. In the middle of all this craziness there is fear and pain in the tears of these people, but though I know that many lives are being destroyed and there is much danger to my body, in my mind I feel safe. The sun is shining, it is a nice day and my instinct says nature will do me no harm. People can harm me, but today everybody is too busy with their own sorry to worry about me.

From the bridge over the Cagayan river we see how high and very strong the water is moving. It looks like it the skin has been pulled off the earth and turned the river brown and swollen so high it is nearly touching the bridge upriver. The landscape is changed. All over the city there are houses washed out with the flood. Many houses at the side of the river are broken and some have disappeared. Banana and coconut and other big trees and two houses are being washed out to sea. One of the trees has caught a man, his body is twisted in a strange way and not moving, I think he is dead. Another lady is washing out to sea. She tumbles and turns in the current, her dress is tangled in her arms and her head is under the water. All around me people are crying coz they are anxious and scared, but the crying and the sad and hurting is not happening to me. I feel as though the warmth of the sun has wrapped me in a cocoon, like I am a chrysalis before it changes into a butterfly and exposed to the desires and dangers of predators.

In a strange way it is exciting to be part of such a big flood, but feeling safe among all this madness seems like madness itself. Like everybody else I understand that my body is in danger, but my mind tells me to be calm that nature will not hurt me. Nature is stronger than men, but I know that men are more dangerous. Nature does not kill from fear or hatred or greed or desire, it is detached from evil. Nature does not care what victims it selects, it does what it always does, nature distributes its power to the strong and the weak indiscriminately and equally. Men hurt only the weak.

I feel the pain of these people and it brings understanding. When I look at all the misery I understand that suffering is not increased when it happens to lots of people, pain is not multiplied by numbers, pain and suffering are personal, they are felt inside each individual. I know from the way I have suffered that a single person can feel all the suffering it is possible to feel.

BD is barking very loudly, she is scared. She is very big and the girls are frightened of her. They give me her leash, but she is a Labrador and too strong for me, I can't hold her and she runs away. Now I have to find her. I was holding her when she ran away so she is my responsibility.

While I am wading through the water looking for BD, the branch of a tree catches on my leg. When I try to push it away I see there is a snake coiled up on the wood. There are many snakes in the bush in Upper Biliran, pythons and small cobras, some bright green ones and other green ones with stripes of many colours. When I was very young I used to walk along small track from my Grandparent's place to my father's small house near the coconut shed and I would often see snakes crossing the path. Always I would stop and stay very still and wait for them to go away. Once I accidentally stepped on the head of a red one. I stepped on his tail then so it couldn't move, but then I couldn't move in case it bit me. One night my father heard the chickens making lots of noise at the back of the house and when he went to look, he saw a very big python there. Its body was as round as my father's leg. He had a gun at that time so he shot it, and the next day my grandmother cooked with *adobo* sauce. I wasn't sure if I should eat this, but when I did it tasted very yummy delicious, like very tender chicken. I don't know if this snake on the branch is poisonous or not, but even if it is not, I don't like snakes unless they are cooked. I stay very still for a few minutes until the flow of the water takes the branch away and I am safe.

When I get to Guisano all my co-daughters are waiting for me. I ask Zelmarie if she has seen BD and 'Yes! He is there with Josierose.'

The housemother tells us that Father Mark and some of the board members are coming to pick us up. She says we will stay at *barangay* High Peak in the seminary with the priests for awhile coz the foundation will need repairs before we can live there again. We wait a long time for Father Mark, but when he comes he won't let me in the car, that I must ride in the back coz I'm so wet. The group in our car is Josierose, ate Merinmae Grace, Pocpoc, Yana, our social worker ate Natasha Pasig and our dog BD who rides in the back with me.

Atty Grace says that before we go to the seminary we will go to her house so we can wash and change our wet clothes. Some co-daughters are already using the bathroom when we arrive, so ate Natasha, Yana and me help Atty Grace to cook chicken *adobo* and rice for breakfast. I eat a lot. After we've done eating I take a bath, but all my things are washed away in the flood and the clothes I was wearing are too wet so Atte Grace lends me a T-shirt and shorts and other things. The worst are her panties, Atte Grace is very fat so her clothes don't fit me, but there is no alternative except to wear her fat ones. Ate Natasha and the co-daughters and staff all laugh at me, but I don't care, I know I look funny. I laugh too coz when I look in the mirror I see that I look like a clown in these sloppy big clothes, but I am happy because everybody is happy. My smile is bigger than my clothes.

When everyone is showered and dressed we go to the seminary on High Peak. Many priests from many counties live here, some from the Philippines, Indonesia, Cambodia, some foreign ones from Europe and America, and also some boys who are studying to be priests. Atte Grace tells Father Mark that I am wearing her extra underwear and Father Mark and the other girls start laughing. I laugh with them and everyone is having fun at my expense, but really I feel very shy coz of their laughter at me. Then Father Mark asks to see my big panties.

'Eeeoow! No way' I say.'

He laughs and laughs then and he starts teasing me so much I punch him in the stomach for making his jokes at me.

When the floodwaters recede next day, our housemother tells us that some of the boys and

Josierose, ate Natasha, Psysy, Sherry, Gayfloreen, Gloryjo, Princess and me, we will go to the foundation to help clean there, and while we are there the other girls will wash the dirty clothes.

The roads to the foundation are all covered in muddy. The only part of the street you can see is where the tyres of the cars have pushed the muddy to the side of the road. When we get to the foundation everybody is so shocked with all the dirty. The foundation is much worse than the streets. In the yard the muddy is drying already and cracking in the sun. When we walk there the mud is so deep it comes over our ankles, in places even it comes up to our calves. Our clothes are still hanging on the line all covered in muddy and some things are even caught up in the branches of the mango tree, but all the flower pots and flowers have fallen down. Inside it is very wet and there is muddy all through the floors of the foundation in all three buildings. Some of the chairs are stuck in the windows, the curtains are all fallen down, the tables are covered in muddy and the refrigerator and the freezer are destroyed. In the storeroom there is nothing that is not covered in muddy. The door to the productivity room is broken and hanging off by its hinges and the productivity room is deep in muddy and lots of dirty. All the tables are turned over, there is only one standing upright. The piano cannot work now coz it is destroyed by the flood, but I think the guitars will be okay coz we put them upstairs. On the wall in the chapel there is a sign saying 'Come Lord Jesus.' This is not touched, and the statue of Mary is still in the same corner place, but all the other things in the foundation are washed out. The flood has destroyed everything and the water has left a wet line on the wall above the doors and windows.

Psysy and I go to our room to check our things. One of the beds is sitting on top of a table. My bed is hanging up on top of that one and some chairs are hanging inside the bed. All my personal things are washed out and this makes me so much sad. My diploma in elementary school and the book with some of the pictures of my dreams I drew for my counsellor are destroyed and these where very important memories to me.

We collect the dirty clothes from all the lockers to take to the seminary house so they can be washed. The boys carry the refrigerator and the freezer outside then we all get spades and start shoveling the muddy into buckets and carrying it outside. When everything is done that we can do for the day we are very dirty, so we wash before riding with Father Mark back to the Seminary.

Every day we clean the foundation and every night we do 'Operation Wash' to clean our dirty clothes. My hands are getting very red and sore because I wash the walls and clean the beds and lots of other things. Three days before Christmas the housemother announces that it is now safe to travel home and spend time with our family for Christmas vacation. Everybody is excited that they will be with our families for Christmas, but the daughters who have no family or the ones who will be in danger if they go home must stay in the seminary. We are to leave the next morning so everybody packs their things. I am to travel early.

After we do our daily rotation of morning prayers, eating breakfast and washing up, I wait for my social worker and Father Mark, they have gone to withdraw money from the bank for the buses. This takes a long time and it is 2pm before they distribute the money.

One week has passed since the flood, but on the way to Iligan, when the bus passes Santa Cruz Chapel by the sea at *barangay* Ojabang, twelve bodies are lying in a line in front of a church. Some policemen are taking measurements and making notes and a priest is making the sign of the cross over them. My nun auntie says that in church you must stand like a candle before God so the bright light of your prayer will rise to him. What is rising here is the smell, and it is so bad it nearly makes me sick that I hold my nose and turn away my head. All the life is gone from these people, all that is left is the smell. When I see them I cannot even tell if they are men or women. These bodies belong to no-one, they are so swollen they don't look like people anymore. The police and the priest are caring for them, but I think God has left this place. All that remains of his dreams are some pretty clothes making the sign of the cross. Will I have to wait to die before someone cares for me?

While I ride the bus my mind wonders, what happens to dead people? Do their spirits live? Do they have minds after they die? Do they remember their lives and have dreams? Do their dreams last for eternity? I hope not. My dreams are not happy, and these people do not look like they are in the heaven that the priests tells us to pray for.

In Iligan I change from the bus to a jeepney. On the way up the mountains we pass one more body that has not yet been collect. It looks so very swollen and black and awful that I worry about my house. My family lives high in the hills, but there is a big lake close by and it is supported by many dams. Sometimes when the rain is very heavy the water flows over the dams and floods the land, but when I arrive at our house I am happy, all is safe. Now I can spend time and days with my family.

Home is a strange place now. I am happy to be here and to be away from the foundation for awhile. The air is clean in the mountains, but the house is windy and smells like smoke, the yard smells like pigs and chickens and mud and rotting fruit. At night the clamour of the crickets and the croak of the frogs croak their way through the holes in the walls. The air is filled with the howl of the dogs, screeching cats and the cheep of bats; they are the smells and sounds of nature. I grew up with these smells, we lived together for many years so they are familiar to my nose, but now I understand that they are the smells of poverty and it causes bitter feelings inside me. When I lived here, I accepted poverty coz I knew no better. My friends and family accept the ugliness; maybe they have filters inside them that sieve out the ragged clothes and hunger. Why should they be gifted this survival mechanism while the hideousness plays out in my mind?

I play and laugh with my friends, but I feel alone. My life is not like theirs. On the outside I am still a little girl, I want to climb trees and play and be silly and laugh and have fun, but inside I feel like a stranger, like some distant relative who has come to visit, someone who is meeting their relatives for the first time. They act nice, but in their eyes I see they feel like they do not know me anymore. Is it them who is different, or me? They are my family and friends, but my experience is not like theirs, they do not know what it is like to be among friends you have known for so long and feel alone. They are happy together, but now I start to understand that their mind lives in a prison. They talk of nothing but putting food on the table and looking after babies. They have no selfish or unfulfilled dreams because they have no dreams, it makes me feel special, but in a way it also excludes me, like a player who gets left out of the game because nobody wants them on their team. I yearn for the days in my memory filled with laughter and smiles, the times before my uncle raped the innocence from my life. Maybe it is good not to have dreams.

Days at home are boring. There is nothing to do at our place now that I have little in common with my friends. My nun auntie takes me to her house again, but she spends all day praying in the church so it is boring there also. I'm glad when this Christmas vacation is finish.

After vacation I return to the seminary coz the foundation is destroyed and still we cannot live there. When I arrive, some of the co-daughters are eating junk food in the store next to the seminary house. They invite me to join them, but I must refuse coz I need to go inside to tell the housemother I have arrived and entertain my nun auntie. When she leaves I join my co-daughters in the store where we eat junk food and drink soft drinks and share stories about our vacations.

I tell them that in Iligan they also experienced typhoon Sendong. I share with them that I saw dead bodies lying on the street and they were decayed and swollen and smelled so bad I had to cover my nose and go away from that place as quickly as possible. Ate Natasha spent a lot of time with her grandmother and celebrated the birthday of her father on Christmas day. Josierose tells us she met her boyfriend from school and they stayed together in the Good-Time hotel. Zelmarie stayed with her boyfriend in the house of his parents. For two days Gennot also stayed in the house of her boyfriend in Kinugetan, and Yana too, she stayed with her boyfriend in the house of his parents. Yana says her boyfriend is very aggressive and wants to sex with her all the time, she doesn't like this. When they are telling me this I start laughing and I cannot stop. All of them are looking at me and asking what is so funny, but I am laughing so much I can't talk to tell them.

Eventually I tell them 'I am thinking of our animals at home when I see them having sex. The *otin* of the pig is so skinny and curly like a corkscrew, but the *otin* of the cow and the caribou is very long and skinny. The horse's *otin* so big and so long that sometimes it hangs on the ground, but the *otin* of the chicken is so tiny that I didn't think they had one, but one day I saw it and it is so small. Sometimes when the dogs are doing sex they get stuck and try to run in different directions, but they can't get apart and we all laugh so much.' I tell these things about the animals, but still I am laughing and say, 'What if one of you got stuck together like the dogs and couldn't get apart? What would you do then? Or what if your boyfriend's *otin* is like the chicken and you can't find it coz it is so small?' Then we all start laughing, but I am laughing so much I cannot even stand up and I fall on the ground.

In the group they share their experiences with, only me and Princess did not stay with boyfriends. Neither of us have boyfriends so we never do what they did. They trust us not to tell, but now I think they don't trust me not to laugh.

I don't like boys. When I am on the bus, boys sometimes say hello and try to chat me, but I never talk to them. Boys put me down all the time and all they want is to sex me. I do have a boyfriend on the internet now. He is a foreigner man, a nurse who works in a hospital in a small town near Perth in Australia. He was married to a Filipina girl here in CDO, but they are separated and he says he is getting a divorce. I have never met him so I don't really know him. We just chat on Face Book sometimes.

At my home I never go out at night, even if I stay at a girlfriend's house I don't go out coz I am scared of the dark and scared of boys. Even if I did go out with a boy I would not make sex with him. I'm too scared of getting pregnant and I am scared of getting infections. My counsellor told me that after I abort my baby someone should make some cleaning in my inside. She told me that if I never clean this then maybe I will get an infection. She wanted to send me to hospital so someone can do this, but I said 'No. I am too scared.' I don't have any infection so I am not letting her send me to the hospital to clean this one. Also she told me that if I am making sex with boys that maybe I will catch an infection from them. I am very scared of having an infection so I would not like to sex with boys.

I the next few days all the co-daughters who were sexing with their boyfriends get scared coz they are afraid they might be pregnant. This makes me worry for them. What if my co-daughters are pregnant? What would they do? None of them knows how to fix it.

Each of them asks me 'how do you make an abortion?' They ask this coz they know that my uncle did this to me, but I don't know the name of the medicine, and even if I did I wouldn't like to tell them, they are too young, Josierose is 17, Yana is 16, Gennot is 15 and Zelmarie is 17. I tell them if they get pregnant they should tell the housemother. When I say this they get very scared. If they tell the housemother then she would tell Father Mark and he would tell the board, then maybe they would be expelled from the foundation and nobody knows what would happen to them.

Life is very unfair. When men do bad things, what they do is their own responsibility and nobody blames them or thinks bad things about them unless they break the law, even then they mostly get away with what they do, but when one woman does something bad, men judge all women and think we are all bad. We are not all like that. I am not a bad girl. I never do those things. I have never had a boyfriend that I sexed with. I never want to do anything like that until I find the right one. Eeeoow! Only my bastard, uncle he did that to me, he is evil and he is too strong so I cannot stop him, but I am not like that.

Zelmarie's menstruation is two weeks late and she is very scared. She tells the housemother and the housemother tells her to wait. She says if nothing is coming soon she will buy a pregnancy test. Next day after Zelmarie's told the housemother, her menstruation came so now we think everything is okay, but it isn't. The housemother told the counsellor and the counsellor told Father Mark. now Father Mark has called a group meeting and he asks all the girls one by one if they commit sexual intercourse on their vacation.

'Not me!' I say. 'I don't have a boyfriend and anyway, I'm too afraid to do this.' Yana, Zelmarie, Josierose and Gennot say yes. When he hears this Father Mark gets very angry mad. 'I never believed you would do this,' he says. 'I thought all the girls in the foundation are scared of sex.'

I am, but many of the girls are not, they like to have boyfriends.

Father Mark says the rule of the foundation is 'The mistake of one is the mistake of all.' He says he is very disappointed with everyone and he storms out of the room in a very angry mood. Now he is not talking to any of us co-daughters.

I ask my co-daughters why they like to have boyfriends. They say they like to love boys coz sometime in the future they will have to leave the foundation and it is too dangerous to go home so they don't know what will happen to them. They say that if they have boyfriends, maybe they will have someone who will look after them. Also that it is fun to have someone to talk to and love who is outside the foundation.

Most co-daughters like to have boyfriends, but not all, some like to have girlfriends. Eeeoow! Now I know why Nellie cut her hair. She and Frances are always together doing things, and sometimes Shiela is with them also. Shiela likes Princess very much, but Princess doesn't like to do that thing with girls. She is like me, she doesn't like to do that thing with anybody.

* * * * *

Some weeks later when the foundation is fixed and clean, we go to live there again, but we can only occupy the first building. The foundation is not the same as it was before, the front has been painted a peach colour, there is a new statue of Mary with flowing water, new sheets, new pillows and new foam for the beds, new coat hangers for our clothes, new trash can, new mirrors, a new TV, computer, fan and emergency light, but the electrical things are not working yet coz there is no electricity. They say it will be one month before electricity comes again to this *barangay*. Also there is no water so we must carry buckets when we wash and flush the CR. Every morning if we take a shower we use mineral water because there is no water in the Comfort Room. Food is OK though coz we cook with gas.

Now we learn about the flood. A big typhoon called Haiyan came from the ocean in the east and when it got to the Philippines they named it Sendong. When it arrived in Mindanao it got caught on Mount Makaturing, Mount Kalatungan and Mount Katanglad and this is where most of the rain fell, nearly half a metre in twenty-four hours. Some companies had been doing a lot of mining in these mountains and had cut all the trees down so when the rain came, some of the mountains collapsed and made avalanches and big mudslides. The water came down the river so fast that the level of the river came up more than three metres in less than one hour. Then the dam controlling the river collapsed and the river level rose almost nine metres. There was also a high tide at that time so the flooding was made worse coz the water could not get out to sea.

This is why it spread so far across the city. All this happened in the middle of the night.

Flooding started at 2:30am. All the houses at the side of the Cagayan River got washed away and many people died because they were asleep and didn't hear the warnings. The people living there who were not killed have no houses now. About one-thousand five-hundred people died, but some held onto trees and wood and things and got washed far away into the ocean. About two-hundred were rescued from the sea. Some people were found on Camaguin Island and this is one hour away by the Fastcat ferryboat. One baby was floating in a Styrofoam ice bucket near Camaguin island and it was still alive. Even today there are lots of people still missing. After the flood there were many dead bodies of people and animals and many people got infected by disease. Some died from this also, but I don't know how many.[6]

Now it is January, one month after typhoon Sendong and another typhoon is coming, its name is Pablo. We all move again to the seminary in case there will be another flood, but it does not happen. After one week

---

6   NB. On Monday October 5th 2015, four year after Sendong, the CDO publication 'Business Week' reported on page 9 that more than 2,000 victims of Typhoon Sendong had still not been relocated into properties supposedly build with donations from the Japanese Non-Project Grant Aid (JNPGA).

in the seminary we go back to the foundation. There is not too much damage, but I am sad, the big mango tree fell down. That mango tree was my friend when I come to the foundation and it shared a lot of my tears.

* * * * *

I am talking to Chemai. She is eleven years old and was raped by her father when she was eight. She tells me this, but when I ask more she won't say anything. She came to the foundation about five weeks ago. When a new girl arrives they mostly don't like to talk. I don't like to talk to them either coz whenever a new girl arrives I get very angry coz now there is another victim. All the time there are victims and each new girl it reminds me that what happened to me never stops, it is happening all the time to other girls.

I am safe here in the foundation, but I am not happy. When I was a child I was happy. I want to be happy again. I was born happy, but my happy past belongs to another me. I like to be happy and I like everyone else to be happy, especially if I make them happy. I love people. I want to trust people even if it's hard to trust them now, but I hate men. Jezel is another new girl arriving in the foundation. She was raped by her father. The men in our country are so bad.

CHAPTER 8

Miscommunication

2013

School intramurals are coming again and all the students are excited to join the games. Intramurals take five days because there are so many events to run. This year I join the Basketball team with Josierose, Yana and Zelmarie. They elect me captain again coz last year I was captain and we won. We have been practicing sometimes in the afternoon, but it is very hot and Yana won't practice. She says that the heat makes all the energy drip out of her. It does the same to us too, but still we practice.

When the game starts, Yana gets the ball, but she doesn't know how to play coz she never came to practice. She thinks all she has to do is throw the ball through the hoop, but she doesn't know which hoop so she runs to the closest one and tries to throw the ball through the hoop at our end of the court. She is so embarrassed coz everyone laughs so much at her. I fall on the ground and I am laughing so much I can hardly play. We win the tournament coz Martha is very good at getting goals. I play defence at the back, but I also get some goals coz at home my father would sometimes play with us and he showed me how to get three pointers.

Fourth year also wins the Dance competition. When we are getting ready for this we have a trainer who comes from outside the school to make the choreography and train us in the afternoons. He makes the routine for us and we learn Hip-Hop dancing. When the competition comes we dress up in costumes and pretend we are on the TV in a show like 'The Philippines got Talent'. This is so very much fun and I think we won coz we are enjoying ourselves so much.

On the last day, everybody gets called up to the stage one by one and we celebrate the awarding of the winners of the games. There is a big sign at the back of the stage that says, 'Talent wins games, but teamwork and intelligence wins championships'. Our volleyball team laughs very much at this coz they elected me captain and I am not very intelligent you know. Also coz Yana never came to practice and we were laughing so much during the game we could hardly play. Really we only won coz Martha is so good at getting goals.

Finally there is a pageant for Mr. and Miss Intramural. One boy and one girl from each level parade in the costume of a cartoon character from TV. All the teachers have a meeting to pick the winner, then they have a prize giving for the winners of all the events they give out trophies.

* * * * *

On Valentine's Day I join the pageant for Miss Valentine. We must all dress up in something we create so I make a gown from a blue curtain. I don't want to wear a dress like this. I do not want to join the pageant, but I do coz the housemother says she thinks I am a lesbian coz I never wear skirts. Lesbians admire beauty and talent and dancing and singing and attractive girls, they are tough and they have girlfriends and do everything that boys can do. If you are a girl you must have relationships with boys. I hate boys. Maybe I am a lesbian coz Nellie kissed me and I like Mary Kate very much, but I could not do things like Nellie and Shiela. Eeeoow! Never would I do things like that.

I join the pageant to show the housemother that I am not a lesbian. I call myself 'Miss Lovable.' I like this name coz in my heart this is what I want to be. In the pageant there is a session for questions and answers. My question is about boyfriends. I cannot answer this question coz I hate boys, so I say nothing. Gennot wins. I think she is not the prettiest, but she is confident in her talking and is good when she speaks the answer to her question.

Next day I ask ate Natasha if I can borrow her extra phone to text Mary Kate. I don't like boys, but I like Mary Kate so I know I am a lesbian, even if I don't want the housemother to know this, but Mary Kate doesn't reply to me.

The phone is bright pink and very nice. Ate Natasha has two phones so she lets me keep her pink one. The next day I receive a text, but I don't know who it is from.

'Who is this please?' I reply.

'This is Jake.' I don't know any Jake, but we start texting each other.

Jake lives in Manila. He doesn't have a girlfriend so he asks, 'would you like to be my girlfriend.'

'Why not?' I say. Jake seems nice and I've never had a boyfriend, so even if it will be a long distance relationship, I think I will try and see what happens. Then Jake sends me 1,000 pesos.

'Why did you send me that?' I ask.

'It's a gift to buy your own phone.'

'OK. Thank you.' I say this coz I don't know what else to say. Boys are very strange.

I use the 1,000 pesos to buy a phone. I pay 900 pesos and I put the other 100 pesos in my locker, but now it's gone, someone stole it. How could they do that? People shouldn't steal. When you steal from people you not only take away their things, you take away their happiness. Happiness is too hard to find, and when you do find happiness, it is only temporary. I never do bad acts and take people's things like that. I don't want to steal the happiness from people. I am too scared to steal and do bad things. I don't want to be arrested and go to jail.

Now all the co-daughters have a problem. There is a new rule in the foundation that we are not allowed cell phones. Father Mark called a meeting and said that some of the girl's grades are slipping and many times the housemother sees the girls crying when they are on the phone. The counsellors told him that too many of the girls are talking to boys on the phone and crying coz the boys are upsetting them. From now on, all phones are banned from the foundation. Any girl who has a cell phone must hand it to the housemother and she will keep it and give it back when we leave. He says that if you need to contact your family you can ask the housemother and she will let us use the foundation phone on the weekend. Some girls hand in their phones, but most don't, we to hide them.

Every morning before we go to school we do our routine assignments like cooking, serving, mopping or washing, then we wait for our transport tricycle. The group in my tricycle is Josierose, Jezel, Yana, Zelmarie and Maricel. When we arrive in school Yana, Zelmarie and me put our things in our classroom and go out of campus. Sometimes we buy load and use our phones. When the bell rings we run back to school for the flag ceremony, we are friends and we are young, I would like to say we are innocent, but we are not coz of what happened to us, but we are having fun.

After classes, Josierose, Zelmarie, Yana and me usually go to the back of the CR under the mango tree. Every day we stay there because there, nobody can see that we have phones. I am a lesbian, but I have boyfriend now so I text and try my best for him, but Eeeoow!!! Boys are so demanding. Always he wants me to be there when he texts. He doesn't understanding that sometimes I cannot answer because I am in class. Eeeoow! It's hard to have a boyfriend.

* * * * *

When we have an outing from the foundation I always wear a cap and I turn it sideways on my head, and when someone takes a picture of me I give a victory sign with my fingers. I feel different, and I like being different. I am a tomboy and I like it, but our outing to Malasag it is very embarrassing for me coz when I am swimming in the pool my teeth fall out.

When I was in elementary school I was playing on a swing, but my friend pushed me too fast and I fell and hit my face on a fence. The fence was made of metal and my front tooth broke. The dentist pulled it out and made me a plate to put in the gap, but when we are playing in the pool at Malasag, my co-daughter hit her head on mine. Two more of my front teeth got broken and I lost my plate in the pool and we don't have any goggles so nobody can find it coz. Now the dentist has taken out my broken teeth and he is making me a plate for three teeth. My eye teeth are so long that when I smile my co-daughters say I look like a vampire. Now I have no front teeth either until they are ready. I cannot laugh or smile for one week and it is very embarrassing, especially coz Jake asked me to send him a picture of me.

He messages me all the time. One time he sends a message asking if I am busy. I am, I want to use the computer to do some study, but it won't start coz the wire to the electricity is broken. It makes me very mad for awhile, but I'm not mad now, I fixed it. The computer is working and I feel very good about myself. The printer is not working though so tomorrow I will try to fix that.

Jake knows that we are not allowed to use phones in the foundation anymore so he wants to know when I am free so he can call. He says he is busy now and will call again after he has finished buying some things for his house. While I wait I put my phone on charge and hide it under the pillow, then go to the first building to help do some cleaning. After we finish, the housemother asks what we would like for a snack. Some daughters suggest tapioca so the housemother asks me to go to the store to buy the ingredients. I am proud to do this. I am proud that she trusts me with money to buy the ingredients. At the store I buy sago, *buko, pandan,* jelly, condense milk evaporated milk, sugar and mango and apple, and I get a receipt. Then I buy some Sun load for my phone coz Jake uses Sun for his telephone provider, not Globe or Smart. I have duel sim cards in my phone so with him I must use Sun so we can text for free.

While I am walking back to the foundation, Jake calls to ask where I am, but I need to drop the call and put the phone in my pocket coz I am near the foundation and no-one can see it when I enter in the gate.

After I list all the ingredients and give the receipt and the change back to the housemother I run to my room to send a message to Jake. I want to tell him that if I can't answer his call it means I am in the kitchen making tapioca for our snack. While I am busy, the other daughters are talking and sleeping so no-one helps me, but I enjoy making tapioca, it is my favourite desert. Ate Natasha taught me how to make it. She usually makes desert, but when she is not in the foundation Yana and I do this.

After it is made I put it in the freezer to cool then run to my room and check if Jake text me. There is no message so I lay on my bed and fall asleep. At 3-o-clock I wake up coz the bell is reminding us that it is time for snacks. I check my phone, but again there is no message. I start to worry then, so I message to ask what happened, why are you not texting me?

When I get to the first building for the snack nobody is eating. Indayjo tells me the housemother said everyone must wait until I arrive. I made the snack so I must serve it, 'We are waiting coz you are late,' she says.

'Sorry', I reply 'I never thought I would have to serve the snack. SORRY!!!'

After I make my apology I distribute the snack to them, but I am not in my mind. I am worried why my boyfriend is not answering my text, but I laugh and pretend to everyone that I am fine.

After our snack the housemother tells me that a light bulb is not working. She asks me to change it. I do, I fix it. For me it is easy and it makes her very pleased. It makes me happy also that I can make her happy.

* * * * *

Josierose wants to meet her boyfriend one the evening. It is not permitted to leave the foundation at night, but Josierose is scared to go alone and wants someone to come with her, so we jump the wall and leave the foundation, but she is disappointed, her boyfriend is not there. We have nothing to do then so we buy some load for our phones and some junk food and come back to the foundation.

I didn't want to leave the foundation at night with Josierose, I am scared of the dark and I am scared of getting caught. When I did this I was in a bad mood. I had an argument with Jake because of Yana. She had no load so she asked if she could use my phone to text her boyfriend, but she sent the message to Jake by mistake. I explained to him that my co-daughter used the phone and sent the message to the wrong person, but he wouldn't listen, he insists that I have another boyfriend. Many times I told him that my co-daughter sent the message, but he ignores me and makes me very mad, that's why I decided to go with Josierose. Now we have a big problem. Yana woke up and saw us jump the wall. She told Gloryjo coz they share the same room together. Then, coz we are always fighting coz Gloryjo won't clean the room properly, she tells the counsellor and today we get a sanction for what we did last night. We have three days of no TV and no computer, we have to wash the walls every day, go to chapel and kneel for thirty minutes every morning to read the bible, and every day for one month we must write down one page of reflection in English and read it in front of everyone in the chapel before prayers. Also, Josierose and I get a strike against us so we have to go to the office and sign that we have a mistake and broke the rules.

Jake and I are talking again. He asks if I can give him a girlfriend for his friend in Manila, but I am not sure about this coz I don't know his friend. 'OK,' I say, 'but only if you give me his number and I will give it to my friend so she can text him.' He gives me the number of his friend Mario and I give this number to Indayjo, but Mario's phone is Sun and Indayjo's is Globe. There are no free texts between different providers so they cannot communicate. My phone has both globe and Sun coz it is duel sim, now I have to relay their messages.

I hate Jake. All the time he is texting and wanting me to answer straight away. Sometimes I am in class and I cannot reply so he is always making trouble for me. He accuses me of having another boyfriend. I don't feel like talking to him when he acts like this so we have been fighting. Eeeoow! Boys are so crazy. But this is not the reason I hate Jake. I went on Face Book and found out he is thirty-five and he is married. He told me he is not married. He is a liar. I told him I never want to hear from him again and I broke up with him.

I hate men, they are such liars. Mario is nice though. I talk to him often when I relay messages between him and Indayjo. Sometimes I express my feelings about why I broke up with Jake; I also told him why I am in the foundation. Sometimes he gives me advice about my life. I never think too much about what he says though coz he is could not really understand. Men could never understand how we daughters feel about this thing that was done to us. Then Mario sends me a message saying 'I love you. I love you. I love you,' and he asks, 'Can I court you? Will you be my girlfriend?'

I am shocked. Mario is forty-two, he was married, but now he is divorced. He is nice to talk to and I am comfortable with him so I say, 'OK. I don't have a boyfriend anymore so why not?' Then Mario sends me 2,000 pesos to buy a new cell phone so he can connect with me every day. I already have a cell phone. Eeeoow! Men are so crazy.

I get a text from Mario almost every hour every day, but sometimes I am in class and when I cannot answer he asks, 'Where are you? What are you doing?' He does not understand that often I cannot answer him coz I am in class. He is crazy like Jake because of this, but he is nice.

We cannot use phones inside the foundation anymore and we must be very careful nobody at school sees them, coz now they are not permitted. The housemother has told us that if they find we have phones they will take them from us. Ailine, Gayfloreen and Gloryjo don't know we have phones and we don't want to tell them. If they know, one of them is sure to report it to the housemother, but Gloryjo sees me with the phone at school and she asks 'Who is the owner of that phone?'

'This belongs to my classmate Jerryvan,' I tell her.

She asks Jerryvan if this is true. He is a good friend and says that the phone is his and that I borrowed it. Gloryjo believes him. Phew! Now my phone is safe again.

Most of the girls in the third building have cell phones. Normally I keep mine under my pillow, sometimes I put it my shoes, or sometimes I wrap it in plastic and put it the flush bowl in the CR, but Gloryjo is having an argument with Gayfloreen at school, so to make trouble for her, she tells the housemother that all the girls have phones. The housemother asks what the colours of the phones are and she says, the phones of Princess and Zelmarie and Josierose are blue, the phones of Marilyn and Yana is pink, mine is grey, but Giselle has no phone. The housemother writes this down.

At the time they are talking we do not know what Gloryjo is doing, coz all of us except Princess are in school, but I receive a text from Princess saying something about Gloryjo and our phones. I cannot understand her text so I go to the class of Josierose and she explains that Gloryjo told the housemother that all of us have phones. This makes me very angry with Gloryjo. Why would she tell on me when she is always borrowing my phone?

When we are on the way home from school I get a text from Princess to say, leave your phone with your classmates coz they might search you when you get back, but it's too late, already we are nearing the foundation.

When we arrive they do not search us, but all the girls are gathering together in the productivity room talking and wondering what will happen. We don't know, so we decide to hide the phones. Yana and Princess put theirs in the rubbish can, but there is water in there so they put it in plastic and cover it over with paper and rags. I hide my phone under the pot where the herbs are growing, Zelmarie and Marylyn put theirs in flower pots also, so now we feel they should be safe, we hope so.

After evening prayers the housemother and EO and the social workers call everyone into the office one by one and ask where our phones are, but no-one answers them. They tell us they know we have phones, but at this stage we are not sure if they do, or just trying to trick us. After all the girls have been called in and asked, everyone is gathered in the productivity room. "We know you have phones,' they say, and they tell us the colour of each phone and who they belong to. Now we know they really do know about them. One by one they send us to get our phones and make us hand the phones over to them.

The EO then gets very mad. 'Why are you doing this when the rule is no phones? You are all bad girls and you can do what you want and I don't care what happens to any of you.' Then she gives our phones back and leaves - Very strange.

We don't know what to do now so we go to our rooms and talk about what just happened. Everyone is angry at Gloryjo, but none of us feel guilty about having phones, because they are important to us. Except for school, phones are the only contact we have with the world outside these walls and without cell phones we can't contact our family and friends, but what is more important is that cell phones are part of being young in our generation. When we are apart we can stay in touch with our friends through Friendster and Face Book and our cell phones help us keep up with technology and this is important. We have computers to use in the computer room and we were allowed to use these for thirty minutes each Friday night and Saturday afternoon, but now this is banned also, we can only use the computers to research assignments from school. Cell phones are the only way we have to keep in touch with our friends and they should be allowed. We have not committed a crime. We are not in jail. We think even prisoners in jail have more freedom to contact their friends than we do. It is not fair that we are kept locked away from the rest of the world. Why should we be punished when we are the victims of what was done to us? We are talking about all this when the housemother and the Executive Officer call us back to the productivity room. 'You must all go and bring your phones here and give them to us,' the EO says.

'Why must we do this?' All the girls are protesting. We don't want to give up our phones and our friends.

'Because now it is against the rules.'

'But this is not fair. We have always been allowed to have cell phones. Why did they change the rules?'

Then they say, 'The board decided to make this new rule because very often some of the girls are getting upset and crying when they are chatting with boys on the phones or on the computers. Too many times you girls are jumping the wall at night to meet boys. You are not doing what you should be doing and focusing on your studies, so the board decided there will be no more access to social media sites on the computer and no more cell phones.'

All the girls are quiet then, coz they know it's true. We have no choice; we get our cell phones and give them up. After we do this all must sign a paper to admit we committed an offence. This is the second time I have committed an offence, but it is not fair. All us girls feel like we are in prison, we are very unhappy about not being allowed cell phones.

March 2013 is the day of our graduation of Blessed Mother College, Fargo. All the graduating students gather in the main building with the teachers and parents and I am one of them. While we are waiting for the graduation, Josierose's mother asks me who Josierose's boyfriend is. She knows that we are friends, but Josierose is afraid of her knowing her boyfriend so I can't tell her, instead I say to Josierose, 'your mother knows you are having a relationship with a boy, so sit your mother next to him so she can get to know him.'

Josierose refuses to do this, she is too scared. Her boyfriend doesn't want to sit next to her mother either coz he is too shy to talk to her.

Our art teacher calls all graduating students one by one to the stage to get our diploma. When she calls my name I am very proud to walk onto the stage. I am so proud to be graduating, especially coz my mother is there to see me. After we get our diploma all the students sing a graduation song called '*The Journey*'. The words are very lovely ...

> *Half the world is sleeping,*
> *Half the world's awake,*
> *Half can hear their hearts beat,*
> *Half just hear them break.*
>
> *I am but a traveller,*
> *Been most everywhere.*
> *Ask me what you want to know.*
>
> *What a journey it has been,*
> *The end is not in sight,*
> *But the stars are out tonight,*
> *And they're bound to guide my way.*
>
> *When they're shining on my life,*
> *I can see a better day,*
> *I won't let the darkness in.*
> *What a journey it has been.*
>
> *I have been to sorrow,*
> *I have been to bliss,*
> *Where I'll be tomorrow,*
> *I can only guess.*

Through the darkest desert,
Through the deepest snow,
Forward, always forward, I go.

What a journey it has been,
And the end is not in sight,
But the stars are out tonight,
And they're bound to guide my way.

When they're shining on my life,
I can see a better day,
I won't let the darkness in,
What a journey it has been.

Forward, always forward,
Onward, always up,
Catching every drop of hope,
In my empty cup.

What a journey it has been,
And the end is not in sight,
But the stars are out tonight,
And they're bound to guide my way.

When they're shining on my life,
I can see a better day,
I won't let the darkness in,
What a journey it has been,
What a journey it has been.

After we sing this song we hug each other and cry
with happiness. Now we have graduated we feel special.

Everyone goes to their parents to have a picture taken. My mother pays for my picture and she doesn't even complain. I am so happy coz it is a very important day for me and I want a remembrance of this happy day I graduate from high school life.

After graduation, all us daughters go back to the foundation with our families where we will celebrate together for two days. I am so proud that my mother and sister and nephew are there. This is the second time she has come to visit me. She came also on the family day four years ago when I first came here. All us co-daughters have prepared a program of music-playing, dancing and singing and a candle parade. Everyone is bonding with their parents, especially at night when they sleep beside us in our room. My sister sleeps in my bed and my mother sleep with me on the foam mattress on the floor.

Next night we have a party and when my one year old nephew is dancing to the music, one of the Nuns gets up to dance with him. All the priests and nuns laugh very loudly when they see this. Later we go to my room to prepare for sleep, but my nephew won't sleep. He plays with Josierose, Gloryjo and Yana until 12-o-clock midnight when he gets too tired and curls up on the bed with my sister, then my co-daughters go back to their rooms.

At 4am next morning the bell rings to wake everyone for morning prayers. Afterward, some of the daughters go to the kitchen and prepare breakfast. My mother and Josierose's mother are washing our dirty clothes and talking and laughing. It makes me happy to see our mothers laughing together. At lunchtime Father Dondon sits at our table to talk with my sister and my mother. He gives me his camera to take a picture of them so I will have a memory of this day. After lunch my mother needs to buy some diapers so the housemother allows us to leave the foundation. While we are at the shop I ask 'Ma can you buy one silka for me?' She surprises me very much coz again she acts like a real mother and gives me money to buy the soap.

On the last morning our housemother refunds the money it cost our parents to visit us, then, while everyone is gathered in the dining room to eat breakfast, I see my mother sitting together and laughing with Josierose and other co-daughters. I don't know why, but suddenly jealousy fills my heart. My mother looks so happy talking to them. She is telling stories and seems to be taking great care to make my friends laugh, but she never cares for me or makes me laugh, she never comes to the foundation to see me like other mothers, she never talks to me or gives me advice or helps me, never do we laugh together. I hate myself for being jealous of my friends, but I cannot rid my mind of the feeling that my mother doesn't like me. She never hugs me or gives me advice and she never makes me feel like I am part of her family. I think maybe it is coz she never breast fed me when I was a baby, so we never bonded. She told me this. My mother would go to work to look after a neighbour's house and I would be left with my grandmother and I would cry all the time until she came back. When I was growing up my mother never hugged me like she hugs my sister, she would always send me away from her.

I feel jealous when I see them laughing and having so much fun together and I hate myself. I never realised until this minute that I hold jealous feelings about my sister. My feelings make me want to cry so I go to the CR where nobody can see that I am alone and not loved. I hate being like this. I hate my jealousy.

My *malata* is packed. My mother will take it home for me. I can't coz I have too many other things to carry. When the mothers are leaving we go outside and wait together until the bus to Iligan arrives. I can wave my mother and sister goodbye and when the parents are gone, all the co-daughters get busy cleaning to bring the foundation back to normal again.

* * * * *

The weekend after graduation we have a prom at the hotel in Limketkai Mall. Seven girls from the foundation are graduating, Josierose, Mariflor, Yana, Zelmarie, Gloryjo, Ailenne and me. My co-daughters wear long gowns, lipstick and make up and they look very pretty. I dress like this also, but I don't know how to choose a dress to suit me so my counsellor helps. We pick a teal blue dress that goes all the way to the floor, but I don't feel comfortable. Usually I wear boy's clothes so in my dress I feel like I am pretending to be somebody I'm not. I pull my hair up like I usually do, but I am too big and the dress is too tight. I think I look like a present that is too big for the wrapping and I do not feel deserving of such fancy wrapping.

My partner is Earl, he is a ladyboy from year three. Some of us have partners from the year below us coz there are not enough boys in our class. He wears black trousers, a black jacket and a brown bowtie and looks very smart. When he is being a ladyboy Earl calls himself Earlaine. He is nice, but also a bit fat like me. I don't like being fat. I think I will get slim again.

For dinner there is Chicken, Rice, fish, chocolate cake and *munchkins* covered with chocolate and coconut. All the girls pretend they are rich, or famous TV stars living in big houses and mixing in high society like Hollywood royalty. It is lots of fun and we laugh a lot, especially with earl coz he acts more like a lady than us girls. I laugh too because we are having a good time, but I am not comfortable pretending like this, I don't know how. I am a simple girl from a simple family. Never have any of my family graduated from school or dressed up in a long dress or disguised themselves behind lipstick and make up. None of my family have ever been to a fine restaurant in a big hotel and had a dinner like this with waiters to serve us. I think that some of the other girls feel the same inside, but they are joking and having fun and looking comfortable as though they dress up and go out like this all the time. So am I, but inside I feel that the person wrapped up in fancy clothes, who is laughing and enjoying herself like

Cinderella, is really just a maid in disguise. I feel like a plastic doll and someone is playing a game with me. I don't belong in this place or in these clothes.

After dinner we have a dance and some picture taking and at twelve midnight our social worker gets a taxi and takes us back to the foundation. The prom is lots of fun, but I'm glad to get out of these clothes.

CHAPTER 9

Resurrection of a Rapist

March 2013

Father Mark calls me into the counselling room coz he wants to talk to me about what course I would like to take in college.

'Criminology' I answer immediately. 'I have thought about this many times' I say. 'I want to study criminology so I can help girls like me and my co-daughters.' This is what I say to Father Mark coz he would not like it if I told him the real reason is that I want to shoot people like my bastard uncle.

Father Mark thinks that studying criminology is not a good idea, that the course is too long. He encourages me to do something shorter. I don't know why he doesn't want me to do criminology, if he is suggesting that I will never finish college then the course I take to start with doesn't make any difference, but I have no choice. The foundation pays for my course until I leave so I have to do what he wants.

I like fixing things. After I fixed the computer, everyone started asking me to fix the lights and other things that go wrong in the foundation so I taught myself how to fix them. I decide to do electrical technology coz I think it will be easy and it makes me feel good to help people. Also, if I do a course with my co-daughters somebody will always be watching me, but if I do a course that nobody else in the foundation is doing hen nobody will be with me and I will have a little bit of freedom. Electrical technology is different; none of the other co-daughters would do this course.

While Father Mark and I are chatting he asks about school and my crushes. I am very relaxed with Father Mark so I share everything with him and we are laughing together.

Then, 'Irene,' he says, 'it is good that you are learning to rely on yourself and you do not do bad things,' and he takes hold of my hands and leans toward me. He moves his face so close to mine that they are almost touching.

Like the eight legs of a tarantula the cold fingers of an uneasy feeling start creeping up the back of my neck. A sense of menace constricts my chest. All warmth seems to have been sucked from the room and it has suddenly become small and dark. My body goes cold. His eyes are growing larger, they reaching out like a magnet that has gripped onto my eyes and won't let go. They are not his eyes, they are glowing like they are on fire. His face is so close to mine I can feel the heat of his voice creaking from the back of his throat. Each word sounds like the door of a haunted house opening on rusty hinges. His words are soft, but they pound like heavy rain on the roof of my mind an send a chill down my spine. In front of me is the mask of a man I once trusted, now I am afraid to look at him. I don't want to strip away the mask coz this means facing the shocking truth of the unknown that lies beneath.

'Who does this face belong to? Who really lives behind this mask? What sins does this mask disguise?' The questions race through my mind. Fear fills my senses. Goosebumps cover my skin. He is talking, but I cannot understand what he is saying. His voice echoes around my mind and get so lost in the black cloud that has engulfed me that I cannot make any sense of what he is saying.

Some crazy man is pounding a drum in my heart - Boom, boom, I hope this talk will be done soon. Boom, boom. How can I get away from here? But still he holds me. My hands are caught in a dry and scaly web. Cold sweat is running down my back. The fury legs of a million tarantulas are crawling over my shoulders. My body cringes from his touch. I see a priest standing over the dead bodies that lay on the road to Iligan. He has a cross in his hands and fire in his heart. Their smell fills the room. With a jerk I pull away like I pulled away from those bodies. I stand and edge toward the door. Father Mark stands and follows me. He takes my arm. My voice trembles when I speak.

'Father' I say, 'I need to go to my counselling session.' I don't have a counselling session. I lie because I am scared of the way he is acting.

'Ah! Okay, then you must go. Your counselling session is important.'

I turn to leave, but he pulls me toward him. He puts his arms around me and hugs me and kisses my forehead and my face. My body goes stiff, under my shirt it is running with icy sweat.

I cannot control myself, my body starts shaking. Somehow I pull the door open and get outside. I run to the first building and curl my body up on a chair in the garage. My mind has left and gone, it is floating somewhere far away. I don't know where, only that I can feel it cringing in the dark corner of some for off place. I am not even sure where my body is coz my eyes cannot see through the monsoon clouds building up inside them. My body won't stop shaking. My mind is filled with loneliness and lost in a darkness full of danger. I am not crying yet. I am trying to be strong, but I am small, I am a child and when I am hurt, I cry. No matter how much I try to grow up, when I am hurt I will always be like a child and cry, it is who I am. It is what makes me, me.

My heart is sobbing. It is dying, but at the same time it is pounding loudly and so fast. It is threatening to burst the dam of my scared and flood my face with tears. My tears are lonely, they want to stay inside, they don't want to spill their sorrow and wetness into this darkness place, it is too big, too cold, too slippery, and I am afraid it will swallow my mind and I will be lost in this dark cloud forever. I need to hold onto something. I pull my knees up to my chest and hold them tight, but I can't control myself, tears fill my nose.

Is it possible to die and for your heart to still be beating? My body is not functioning. I feel like I am dead. I cannot even hear the voice calling my name. Only when Indayjo punches me hard on my back does my mind come into my head again.

'What is the matter with you? What happened?' she asks

I share with her my fear of Father Mark.

'Don't mind, she says 'there's nothing you can do.'

Talking to Indayjo calms me down. She is right, I am trapped in the foundation for awhile and there is nothing I can do. I agree, and after talk awhile the tears stop. My heart it is still raining and flooding me with sadness, but now it is only inside.

When Indayjo and I stop talking I go to the *sala* to get a snack and watch TV with the co-daughters. A short while later Father Mark passes to go the housemother's office. When he returns he says goodbye to everyone, but I cannot look at him. He rubs my head when he passes, but his touch makes the hair on my neck bristle and my skin feel itchy. I nod, but my mouth is locked as tight as the doors of a prison, it will not open to make words of any kind.

* * * * *

We are going on vacation tomorrow, but my sleeping is not good. The co-daughters in my room wake me coz I am shouting and fighting and punching the air. They say that while I am sleeping I am holding my hand over my mouth and kicking and fighting. This time I remember. I am dreaming my uncle is holding me down and trying to kiss me.

* * * * *

When I arrived home for my vacation my friends in Upper Biliran have changed. We laugh and we play and we talk, but in the contented look of their eyes I see their future. They have no desire to leave this place, no want to pursue an education or experience the wonders of the world or to live any dreams or do anything different than they do in this forest. Each day I watch them wake contented from their dreamless sleep. All they want is a baby and a man, but men are bad, and now I see that babies will root them in poverty and their lives will never change.

After a few days my father gets a call on his phone and calls me. 'Someone wants to talk to you,' he says.

'Who?'

'I don't know, maybe a friend from CDO' he says.

When I hear the voice at the end of the phone the hair bristles on the back of my neck and my stomach falls out of my body. It is the voice of my uncle and his words roar in my mind.

'Why are you calling me?' I demand.

'Because I need something,' he says. 'I want to work abroad, but I can't get police or NBI clearance from the National Bureau of Investigations. I have a bad record there. I need the papers you signed to say you stopped the case so I can get a clearance.

'Sorry,' I say 'but the papers you need are not with me and I don't know where they are.' My voice is cold. I do know where the papers are, the Piscal has one copy and my mother has the other, but I will never give them to him.

'Anyway, you are wasting your time. I have a lot of things to do that are more meaningful to me on my vacation than talking to you, but you call me and you have spoiled my vacation. You are wasting your time calling me. I will make sure those paper are never put in your hand. All the time you want to go overseas and can't go, I want you to remember that it was me that stopped you. I want you to feel what I feel all that time you raped me.'

I say this, then I off the phone. I feel so much anger toward him. He is the worst bastard uncle I ever know in my whole life. Damn!! Damn!! Damn!! Shit!!

After I talk to him I give the phone back and my father asks 'Who is that man calling you?'

'It is just some stranger wanting to know me' I say.

He raises his eyebrows and the temperature of his voice drops. When he speaks again he is in a bad mood. I am in a bad mood also. I run to my room and lock the door and cry. I know my father knows who it is and I can't understand why he would let my uncle talk to me and not even warn me who is on the phone. My bastard uncle stole my childhood. I just wanted to be a little girl Hand grow up with my friends and be happy. I just wanted to feel loved and be part of my family, but that bastard made me feel like and animal. Damn!!! Damn!!! Damn!!! I hate him. I am not an animal.

My mind is confused and tormented. I cannot understand why my father would give me the phone and let my uncle talk to me like that. I cannot understand why my father does not protect me even a little bit from feeling so much hurt. My mind is filled with thoughts of how I can take revenge on my bastard uncle? Revenge, revenge, my mind keeps thinking about revenge. I think of all the girls in the foundation who have been raped and I cannot understand why we have to suffer while the killers of our childhood walk free and go abroad to work while we are kept locked in a prison without even a cell phone to communicate with our friends. Bad thoughts hurt my mind until I am so tired I fall asleep.

When I wake I don't want to leave my room. My uncle calls many times to ask me for the papers, but I refuse to talk to him. My uncle has ruined my life and he is ruining my summer vacation and my father is helping him. I hate my bastard uncle and now I don't know what to feel for my father. I can't hate him coz he is my father, but I cannot trust him to look after me. I feel very alone, like there is nobody who cares for me and will protect me.

When I go back to the foundation I am still very angry. Many days have passed since my uncle put this burning in my mind, but darkness lives inside me and the anger remains. My mood won't change and I cannot fix it. I don't wait for the day of my counselling session, straight I go to the office of my counsellor to tell to her what happened and express what I feel.

'Revenge is a bad idea.' She says that if I think of revenge all the time then bad things will take over my mind, that bad thoughts are like weeds in the garden of the mind and I must replace them with flowers.

I don't understand this. Flowers need sunlight to grow. I don't know how flowers can grow in my mind when it is so dark and hurting in there. She always advises me about my life, she says that when I am mad at someone I should talk to them: she says I am shy because I won't let the past leave my mind, she says I must love myself, that I should regularly go to confession and that I should listen to myself and decide if I am a boy or a girl. I do not understand many of the things she wants me to do, her words are very confusing.

After talking to her I feel exhausted. Sleep was not my friend on this vacation coz my bastard uncle filled my mind with hurting and anger. I go to my room and lie on my bed. My eyes are watching the ceiling, but thoughts of what I can do to make revenge on my BASTARD, DAM, DAM uncle will not leave me Like I do every night I toss and turn and search for somewhere my mind can be at peace, but sleep won't come, and even if it does I know it will not be good.

This night I dream my uncle is coming to the foundation to get the papers he needs. I am so scared that my fear wakes me up and my nose runs with tears all night. The dreams are so real and fear grips my chest so tight that many nights I try to shout the scared away by screaming into my pillow. Every night my bastard uncle is here in my dreams. I shout in my sleep. I jerk all over the bed. My co-daughters are so frightened they wake me many times. When they do this it makes me very scared coz I remember my dreams. Sometimes my uncle has a big knife and is coming to kill me. Saliva runs from his mouth: his claws hold me down, his teeth are filed to a point and stick out like the fangs of an *Agta*. I struggle and fight coz I don't want to die. He is evil for me.

When your heart is full with fear it is hard to go to sleep, but waking up is harder. When the lights come on it is hard to open my eyes. I feel my sheet drowning in the tears that fear chases from my eyes. He is the devil and I am scared. I am too young to die. There must be good dreams in my mind somewhere, but for now they are buried in the cellar and covered with mud and my uncle has slammed the door shut, but I know they are there. I feel that somewhere inside me they are like buried seeds waiting for the rain to stop and the sun to shine so they can grow. But all the time I feel like I am nothing and my life is a misery. I have nothing, but my life. I want my freedom and I want to live.

Sometimes my mind runs away. When this happens my co-daughters punch me. They know a punch works to bring my mind back into my head coz sometimes they need punching also. Their punch wakes up my mind a bit, it jerks me back to reality like a leash on a dog that gets pulled back when it tries to chase another dog, but these days I cannot stay in my mind. Many times I don't answer when someone speaks to me

My time now is always bad. When Father Mark is there he acts very strangely toward me. Always he is poking me with his finger in my stomach or on my shoulder, sometimes even on my *totoys*. He laughs when he does this, but it is not funny to me. Now when he comes to the foundation I am not comfortable and don't sleep well, when he is not there I feel more comfortable.

When I look in the mirror I cannot see myself. All I see is a hologram that has been stripped of my youth and my innocence. Not only has my body been raped, but my mind and my personality have been scarred for life. Because you cannot see scars it does not mean they are not there.

*   *   *   *   *

The rules of the foundation have changed again and the housemothers are being very strict with the new rules. Every time we are going to or coming from school someone checks our school bags looking for junk food or cell phones or cameras. None of these are allowed in the foundation anymore. There is no wearing of sleeveless shirts or shorts, even in the rooms: unless we are sick we are not allowed to sleep except at siesta time, there is no TV on Sunday coz it was in the agreement everybody must sign when they come here. Now there is nothing to do and everyone is bored. Some of the co-daughters speak to Father Mark about this. He says he disagrees with the rules, but he will not interfere, the rules are set by the housemothers.

Rules for the New Foundation

No cell phones. Calls can be made
to our family on the housemother's
phone, but only on the weekends
No Face book.
No steady boyfriends.
Not allowed to wear shorts or singlets.
Not allowed to wear short dresses or
high heels.
Not allowed to go to other girls rooms.
Not allowed to borrow other person's
things.
Not allowed to wear nail polish.
Not allowed to cut classes.
Not allowed to take drugs.
Not allowed to take pregnancy tests.
Not allowed to talk to people over the
fence.
Not allowed to drop subjects from
school.
Not allowed drinking alcohol or
smoking cigarettes.
Not allowed to leave the grounds of
the foundation unaccompanied.
No TV on Sundays.

But the biggest rule is that if you make three mistakes you will be expelled from the foundation. This is very harsh and the girls are very frightened of this rule. If they get expelled many girls have nowhere to go.

CHAPTER 10

Religious People do not live in this world

June 2013

I have been thinking about my young years in Upper Biliran and all the things I used to do with my friends. When I was a child I was sickly and accident prone. In grade one of elementary school I got ringworm infections. Big holes came to both my cheeks and thick, white liquid like condensed milk formed in them. My parents had no money to send me to the doctor so they got amoxicillin powder from the pharmacy and each morning and night they put it in the holes and bandaged them with some special crushed leaves my father gathered from the forest. After about five months the holes went away. When my brothers and I were riding a caribou, I fell off and smashed my knee on a rock and for a long time I couldn't walk. Many times when I was playing or opening coconuts I cut myself with the *sundang,* and once I fell out of a guava tree and two large splinters lodged in my armpit. The doctors wanted to operate to take them out, but there was no money to pay for an operation so my arm swelled up very big. Then one day when I was playing with a friend he accidentally squeezed it. Lots of pus and blood squirted out and a hole came so big that I could see the splinters, so I pulled them out. After awhile it healed.

Things were not all bad though, when I was twelve I loved to go swimming with my friends in the pool at Maria Christina falls. We would go in the afternoon and stay until evening. I loved to watch the sun going down and its fingers reaching up to paint the sky. Sometimes they would be painted orange and sometimes crimson red. I liked red in those days, coz red is so bright it felt like a splash of happiness against the everyday greens and browns of the forest. I would dream that someday God would teach me to paint like him and I would be able to make colours as beautiful as the sunset. I would sit with my friends in the high branches of an old tree by the falls and we would pretend the last rays of the sun were our boyfriends winking at us through the leaves. None of us had boyfriends. We were too young to care about boys. We talked about them sometimes, and about what love would be like. My life now is not like I dreamed it would be when I was a little girl. When I was young I dreamed that the first boys I kissed would be my love for the rest of my life, but boys didn't matter then, we didn't care about them except as friends, we were just pretending to be grown up.

Sometimes if we were late, the stars would come out while we walked up the three hundred and thirty steps leading from the pool to the path winding through the coconut plantation. The stars would be so bright we would pretend they were mangos hanging from the sky and we would jump high and try to pick them. The stars have been travelling around the sky forever, they have grown old with their wandering, but they are still young enough to be friends to young children.

I learned to swim in the pool beneath the falls, but not when it is raining coz the water is very cold, and if the rains come too heavy and the water flows very strong, people sometimes drown. Going to the falls and playing with my friends was always a special time for me. When I was young life was as sweet as the honey we would sometimes find in the trees.

An older sister of my friend told me that the Maria Christina Falls are named after two sisters who fell in love with the same man. They were good sisters to each other and neither wanted to take the man away from her sister, so they agreed they would commit suicide together by jumping off the top of the falls. There is a big rock in the middle of the falls and when the water parts around the rock it looks like the long hair of the two sisters cascading into the pool. When I was young I thought, why would anyone want to do that, why would anybody want to commit suicide. Now I know there are many reasons people do this

* * * * *

College has started. I have joined the class in electrical engineering. It is exciting, but very scary coz there are thirty eight boys and I am the only girl, but the boys are very nice to me. I made a list of all the things the teacher says I need for the class and I gave it to the EO. She says she will buy them for me.

I am proud to be in college. I feel like I am growing up. I am happy, happy, happy this day, but there is a big problem. My counsellor ate Lorraine asks me if I have a phone.

I said 'yes.'

She raised her eyebrows when I said this. 'Where is it?' she asked.

I took my phone out of my bra and put it on her desk. She looked at the calls from all my friends and my boyfriend. She knows I am not supposed to have a phone, but after she looked at the messages she gave it back and said, 'Don't let anyone else see this.' Ate Lorraine is very nice, she is not the big problem. Before dinner all the staff had a meeting. After dinner Father Mark announces that we all must go to the *sala* to watch TV together and no-one is allowed to go to their room.

This is not normal and a sudden sense of foreboding started to grow in my chest. I feel like something bad is going to happen. What will the staff do? My guess is that they are going to search the rooms for phones. I get scared, my phone is folded inside the clothes in my cupboard. Sometimes I put it in my shoes or wrap it in plastic and put it in the flush bowl in the CR, but now it is folded in my clothes in the cupboard so it will be easy to find.

Yana has hers folded in her underwear in the cupboard like me and Zelmarie has her phone under her pillow. Josierose has her phone in the bag in her room and she is very scared. Already she has been caught one time having a phone and had to sign to say she has a sanction. Normally we keep them in our pockets, but today we hid them because Father Mark told us we would be watching TV after dinner and we thought that they were gathering us together to search us.

Father Mark says, 'Someone must wake up Marylyn and tell her to come to the first building.' Immediately I volunteer.

When I wake Marylyn, I tell her she needs to hide her phone coz the staff might be checking our things soon. She puts it in the trash can. Then I go to the other room to find Jezel coz she is in bed with a fever. 'Hide your phone' I tell her, so she also puts it in the trash can.

After I return to the first building, the staff go to the rooms to check our things. Me and Zelmarie are holding each other so tight I can feel her shaking. She is very nervous coz she has her phone under the pillow and they will easily find it there. I am very nervous for her also, but when I look at ate Natasha she is so relaxed. She is the only one that has her phone in her pocket so she knows they cannot find it.

The staff check all the rooms and we are very surprised coz they find nothing. Then Jelissa goes to the room of Princess to get a comb. The housemother sees Jelissa open the bag of Princess so the housemother sends Jelissa out of the room and looks in the bag,

She finds Princess' phone. Princess is then called to the office and the housemother asks about her phone. Princess keeps her eyes down and her mouth shut and says nothing. The housemother confiscates her phone and she gets a sanction for breaking the rules, now she will have to get another phone. When we go back to the rooms all our things are arranged all neat like we left them, we are very surprised.

All the daughters like the housemothers and the staff, but these days there is a separation taking place, a barrier is forming that places them on one side and us daughters on the other. The new rules are too harsh. The girls are bored coz there is nothing to do and nothing to make any excitement for us. We want a connection with normal people who live outside the foundation, but all of us are frightened. If we are caught breaking the rules three times we will be sent away, and where would we go. Some girls have families they can go to, but many don't.

Ate Natasha is the only one who is not worried. She is very nice and helpful to me and we are good friends, but my counsellor does not like ate Natasha. One time when the counsellor came to the room, ate Natasha's phone was ringing and the message was from Father Mark. We all saw it. Father Mark knows she has a cell phone, but he ignores it. She is his favourite coz he knows her family from Dipitan City. The priests have a congregation there and her family goes to the church with them. He says she is a role model for us girls. I told my counsellor about ate Natasha's phone and how Father Mark ignores it.

'Yes,' she says. 'I know already that she has a phone. I know it is unfair for Father Mark to have a favourite. I don't like it either, but there is nothing I can do.'

* * * * *

Father Vegas is not like Father Mark, he is very nice to everyone. He hugs and kisses me, but I am not frightened coz he hugs and kisses all the girls, and the housemothers and the counsellors. He is very fat and has many lines on his face like old people, but his lines are happy lines coz he is always laughing. He is very funny when he laughs coz his tummy bounces up and down and he looks like Santa Claus going over bumps on his sleigh.

'Laughter is exercise for the insides.' He always says this. He lives in Vietnam, but he often comes to visit the girls in the foundation; he was the priest here for seven years before I arrived.

When I hear that Father Vegas is in town I text him and ask if we can meet so I can talk to him about a problem I have. He texts back to say I should meet him at a Vietnamese restaurant in Guisano Mall. He likes Vietnamese food very much. He knows that I do not like to meet any man if I am alone, even Father Vegas, so he tells me a friend of his will be with him, but if he has a friend with him I cannot meet him. What I want to talk about I do not want to discuss in front of a stranger.

'I will come to the seminary later when I finish college,' I tell him.

This is my last semester in the foundation and I tell Father Vegas that I don't like this world and I don't want to be here anymore. I want to give up and get away from everything. I tell him I don't want to go back to Upper Biliran when I leave the foundation, but I have nowhere else to go, so maybe I will commit suicide. 'What I really want is to study, but there is no way for me to do this.' This is what I tell him.

'Where will you live if you don't go home?' Father Vegas asks, but I can't say, I don't know.

'Who will support you if you study?' he asks.

I have no-one to support me. All I can say is, 'I don't know.'

'Then you must pray.'

Father Vegas always says this to the co-daughters if they are lonely and scared and don't know what to do. I have pleaded with God many times, but he does not listen. God is deaf to my pleas.

Father Vegas is a good man, he is kind and he does many good things, but now I see myself as he sees me. I see that I am not a real person. I am a good deed, a little girl he can make happy for a while so he can fulfil his obligation to God and go to heaven. I hate myself for thinking like this, coz Father Vegas is very kind, but what else can I think? We learn about doing good deeds and going to heaven every morning and afternoon and every Sunday when the priests make sermons at us. I do not like this praying and going to church, but I must coz it is a rule of the foundation and they are caring for me now, but religious people do not live in the same world as real people, it is not possible to talk to them or ask them for help. Everything bad that happens for them has the same fix, 'You must pray.'

Always Father Vegas tells us girls we should pray if we have a problem, but this day when he says you must pray, I feel the floor falling away and I am left dangling in empty space. I cannot control myself, my legs start shaking and tears come to my eyes. I don't want to go back to Upper Biliran. I don't want to suicide. I have been raped too many times in too many ways to now be raped of my future. My time in the foundation is racing toward and end rolling clouds of a super typhoon, it is threatening to drown me and it seems like nothing can stop it. I want to live. I need help. I beg.

'Father Vegas,' I say, 'I feel that praying does no good. My relatives in Upper Biliran are bad and I am in danger there. I feel there is nothing to hope for anymore and maybe I will just give up and suicide.'

Father Vegas has never seen me cry, he has only ever seen the happy Irene coz when he comes in the foundation I am always joking and laughing, but now the scared Irene is bringing out the tears and I cannot stop her. Father Vegas puts his arms around me and hugs me. I feel my fingers cling onto him like I want to hold onto my father, but even that I cannot do. Never can I hold on to my father and hug him. He never does that to me. Sometime he hugs my sister, but never to me. My father is not like that with me.

It feels good to have Father Vegas put his arms around me, but there is a cold storm building inside me. There is rain pouring from my eyes. I am alone and adrift on a river of pain and hopelessness and my grip on Father Vegas is the only thing keeping me afloat. I hold Father Vegas tight and cannot let go, even when I see the rain running off my nose and falling on his jacket I cannot let go to wipe it away. I am lonely, and loneliness is a terrifying adventure, it locks shut all the doors to happiness. I am afraid, and my fear drains me of thought. Father Vegas holds me until there is no more rain, but the emptiness and loneliness and fear do not go away.

A distant voice is saying, 'Maybe when you leave the foundation the priests can help you. You must never give up your life. No matter how bad things get or how bad you feel. You must pray and never give up.'

He is always telling us girls to pray, but he does not come from where I come from. He does not see the drooling face of my rapist uncle hovering over him every night. He does not wake up scared to open his eyes in case the rapist has escaped from the dream and is standing beside my bed. His life is fortunate. Living brings him no harm. He comes from a place where the wind does not blow through the boards in the walls and the streets are not made of dirt, he lives where there is always food on the table and people who love you to share it with, were you do not have to draw water from a well, he lives at the top of the tree where the fruit is juicy when it ripens. I live where worms crawl and the roots of the trees grow out of mud and many times there is no food to eat. He does not understand that when he tells me to pray, he is not helping me. I say this to him.

'To pray is to hope,' he tells me.

I don't reply. I don't understand. I do not know how hope can help me. If hope is real then it only happens in his world, it is only real for people who have a future. My life is happening in a world of hunger and loneliness and danger and fear, and these are like dark, heavy clouds that make my heart hurt and my eyes blind coz they are always raining.

When I leave Father Vegas he gives me three Toblerone chocolates. I like Toblerone chocolate so I feel happy. I also feel happy that we talked and I shared my problems, but he has not helped me. I have been in the foundation for nearly five years and soon I have to leave. In front of me is a big wall and beyond it is a darkness place. This is my last semester in the foundation and I have nothing to hope for or any way to solve my problems.

* * * * *

In my course in college I am elected the *beadle,* this means I am secretary to the teacher. It is my job to check the attendance and record the scores of the tests for all my co-students. All the boys are very nice. They call me Princess. They help me do my demonstrations of electricity and help if I forget to do my homework because I am busy in the foundation. We eat together and go everywhere together. They have created a new world for me and even if it is only temporary, I am happy living here.

* * * * *

I don't know how he found out where I am, but whenever I go on Face Book now there are messages from my uncle.

'Hi,' He says 'how are you? Where are you now?'

He wants to come and see me. I think there must be no feeling inside him for other people. Does he have no idea how much I hate him for what he did? I think he does not even understand that what he did is wrong.

I never answer him. I never want to see my bastard uncle again. I block him and I change my Face Book account many times, but always he finds my new one and messages me again. I block him again and again, but it makes no difference. To me he is the face of evil. I think that his contacting me is the fault of my nun auntie's coz she did not want me to continue the case against him. She cannot see what is in front of her eyes. She cannot see the right and wrong of what she did. All she sees is a man on a cross, she sees his suffering and she prays to him, but for me it is the wrong man on the cross, it should be my bastard uncle who is nailed there and suffering. Can she not see my pain, or does she see only what she wants to see.

* * * * *

This time when Father Vegas comes to visit the foundation and hugs and kisses all the girls I pull away, but he grabs my hair and pulls me to him and hugs and kisses me. When I feel his belly bouncing up and down it makes me laugh and he laughs with me. I am not afraid of Father Vegas, he is very nice and he acts like a real father to all the daughters. Today he gives me advice about my life. Someone must have told him about Jake or Mario coz he tells me I did wrong and I made a mistake to have a boyfriend while I am in fourth year high school, but I think that maybe he is not always right. My boyfriend is far away in Manila and we are only text friends, I have never met him, but I need a boyfriend. I have nobody else and if I don't have a boyfriend, who will look after me when I leave the foundation? My family cannot do this, my life and outlook is different to their experience and they have no money to feed another person. My nun auntie cannot be doing this, she only prays and protects my uncle. The foundation looks after me now, but my five years will soon finish and I will have to leave. I have no money and no work, I have no education or degree and now the only places I have to live are both darkness place that are full of judgment and danger, so who will look after me when I leave? When you have nothing else in you life, why is it so wrong to have a boyfriend? How can people get to like each other and get married and make a life together if they cannot have boyfriends? People of religion are very confusing. Sometimes they do good things and help others, but they have very strange ideas about some things. They do not understand the feelings of real people.

When I feel lost like this, I sometimes search through my mind trying to find reasons why people do what they do. Now I think I understand why people who have religion are always happy, they do not have to look after themselves and make themselves safe. God is not good to everyone, but people who believe in religion, like Father Vegas and my nun auntie, they always have somewhere to live and someone to look after them, they do not need to take responsibility for themselves. They do not understand what it is like to feel helpless and scared and trapped in a dark corridor leading nowhere. Always they have somewhere to live where they are safe. But I think God does not give them this safety; people like my mother and father give it to them when they give money at church, and they get help from government officials and big companies like the Delmonte Corporation.

My nun auntie never lets me be safe. I do not fit under the halo of her protection. Only she protects her evil brother. She is a nun and she is good coz she is a nun, but when she protects her brother I think that she puts her halo aside and does evil. Sometimes I think her god is evil. I am not sure about God. They tell us in religion lessons that God sees everything, and knows everything, and God is good to everyone. But if God sees everything and knows everything then God must be a man, coz only a man god could let such bad things happen to us girls. My auntie goes to church every day, but hanging from a tree makes you a mango, and going to church does not make you good.

My nun auntie found out I had a crush on Mary Kate and now she is says that if I do bad things, like being a lesbian or dressing in shorts and having boyfriends, then I must ask God's forgiveness and if I don't, then God will make me burn in hell forever. She tells me this so many times I think *she* is scared of burning in hell. But why would God do that to anybody if he is good? Good people don't burn people, and good people don't scare others children with such stories. What she tells me is very frightening. I cannot understand why would she tell me such stories and make me afraid of more things than I am already afraid of? Perhaps this is why she believes in God, he is the only one who can understand. Maybe she has a faith that lets her believe she can do anything she wants, that all her actions are good and she will never be punished no matter what she does, coz all she needs to do is ask forgiveness and she will be forgiven, but I must keep these thought about God in my mind and not say them to anybody. The priests and the counsellors would not like to hear me to say these things.

* * * * *

My uncle has found me again. He is contacting me on Face Book so this time I do reply, I post a message on his Face Book account. I write it in Tagalog and in English so everyone can read it.

'You are a rapist Freddy Rebusto. You raped me when I was thirteen. I am your niece and you are supposed to look after me, but you raped me many times. You are evil and if you keep contacting me I will re-open the case against you and you can rot in jail.'

A few days after I post this my nun auntie contacts me. She is very angry and demanding, 'Why did you do that?' she asks.

Why is she angry with me? All I want is for him to stop contacting me. Why does she blame me? Why does she protect him? I am thirteen years old when her bastard brother raped me. Many, many times he did this. She has taken sides with the devil. She is a nun of the Christian religion and she helped him to get away without being punished for his sins. I do not understand this. I do not like my nun auntie. She is not a good nun. She does not do good things. She helps her brother and when he contacts me it makes his evil stay in my mind. Does she not understand that I have feelings like any other person? It was her that first put it in my mind that I am bad. I am not bad. I was just a little girl and I was innocent. All I wanted was to grow up with my family and for my family to love me.

When my nun auntie was young she was in love with a man, but he left her and married someone else and this broke her heart. No boy could ever break my heart, my uncle and my family did this long before any boy had the chance.

I think my nun auntie found her religion coz she could not have her boyfriend. When she was young she got so lonely she gave up on life and is hiding behind an addiction to God. Love is hard to find, but loneliness is easy, it is everywhere. I think you can find loneliness in any community, but still I do not understand why she protects my uncle and not me. Why did she make me drop the case against my uncle when he is also a man? She must know what it is like to be in pain, she must know how I hurt. If the pain of a man caused her addiction to God, maybe she is trying to increase my pain so I will join with her in her addiction, but I do not want to be an addict to anything, especially God. I think that inside she is miserable and misery likes company.

I tell my auntie, 'You are always putting me down. This is my life: I am an adult now and I am the one who will decide what to do with it.' She did not like it when a said this to her.

CHAPTER 11

Courage Cannot Exist Without Hope

July 2013

Mario is annoying. Sometimes when he texts he calls me honey. I have told him many times I don't like this, but still he does it. Now he tells me he wants to come to CDO so he can meet me on my birthday, but I went on Face Book and discovered he is courting other girls. His ex girlfriend Ariana is in CDO and he is also coming to see her. I terminated the relationship today. I told him he is a liar and I never want to hear from him again.

* * * * *

All the boys in college are very good to me. Now I have broken up with Mario, some of them suggest we should get drunk, so after class we go to the *Calandaria* bar in back of the college. Troy's girlfriend broke up with him and he is also sad. Troy is always kissing me on the cheek; I think he has feelings for me. Every time I go somewhere he seems to be there, and when he sees me he always offers to carry my things for me.

At the *calandaria,* five of us drink four big bottles of beer and when we finish drinking I cannot see straight and all the world seems to be spinning round and around my head. This is funny and makes me laugh, coz really the world is spinning around, but I have never seen it spin like this before. Now I can see it happening and when I tell everybody they laugh so much.

I get a jeepney to the foundation, but I am so drunk that when I get out of the jeepney I fall down in the middle of the street and start crying. Even if he is a liar I am still sad and broken hearted to break up with Mario, now I have nobody.

Princess comes home and sees me sitting in the street crying with all the cars passing around me. She helps me stand up and takes me into the foundation. 'You must have a bath and clean your teeth, you smell like beer,' she says.

I am lucky, all the housemothers are at evening prayers so nobody sees me, but when I lie down, my bed is spinning like a *Kasing* and I feel very sick. Next morning there is big thunder in my head and it feels like it wants to explode like volcano. I wish it would. This is my first time to get drunk and the feeling is so bad I will never do this again.

The boys paid for the beer for me coz I have no money. In high school we are not allowed money: we were given biscuits and food for lunch. In college we get ten pesos each day. I saved my money secretly and bought a T-shirt for fifty-nine pesos. I bought one for Indayjo also, but now I am in trouble with the housemother again.

'Where did you get that new T-shirt?' she demands, but I don't answer.

'Where did you get the money,' she demands, but I cannot tell her. I can't tell her I saved my money coz we are not allowed to save our money and we are not allowed to buy things like T-shirts. What does she expects me to say? Everybody must have the same clothes. They say that if we have different things some of the girls get jealous, especially the young ones in elementary class. The housemother lets me keep the T-shirt, but now she is not talking to me.

* * * * *

Princess's birthday is on September 17th so on that day she and Josierose and me go to Guisano and buy a birthday cake from Red Ribbon. Her boyfriend buys the cake. Josierose and I have saved our ten pesos each day and we buy one gallon of ice cream, but one gallon is too much, even four of us.

* * * * *

I think I am old now. My years are young, but sometimes my mind seems to be getting old. When I talk to my college friends we laugh and joke, but the way they act is like children. I want to be a part of them so I act childish as well, especially when I joke with them, but inside I feel different. There is a memory that is an open wound festering like an ulcer in my mind and it will not scar. My school friends have no thoughts about things like rape or abuse or loneliness, they have no knowledge of things like this so when we talk, the subjects never come up. It is nice to be having friends who are normal people. When I am with them my scar is not so colloid.

My mind is getting old, but so is my body. Grey strands are coming into my hair. My grandfather has a full head of hair even at his very old age, but it is all silver grey. He told me it turned grey when he was very young. When I look in the mirror now there are many grey strands like my grandfather's running through my hair. I thought there would be more to life before it got old and turned grey, maybe I have already experienced more of life than many old people ever do.

Today I am reading a book and in it one of the characters says *'Courage cannot exist without hope'*. The words reminded me of what Father Vegas said about hope, and it makes me think. When I look it up, the dictionary says that hope is an expectation that something good will happen in the future, but I have no future so where can I find a hope that something good will happen in it. When I leave the foundation I will have nothing, no education, no love, no money, not even ten pesos a day, all I will own is fear. Father Vegas says prayer is like hope. He also says prayers are like wishes, but he never feels what I feel. Hoping and wishing cannot give me rice to eat, they cannot give me an education, hope and wishes cannot protect me from my uncle, with hope there must be a path to gain what you want, and food to give you strength to follow that path.

How do people get strong? What gives people courage without making them evil like my uncle? How do they feel secure and find love and get the things they need? How do they make their lives safe and happy? These are questions I ask so that I can make wishes and have hope, but nobody can give me the answer, only they say I must pray. I think hope is like a dream, it seems real, but really it is a fantasy.

One time in my home there was a typhoon and after the typhoon my I found a *maya* bird with a broken wing. When I held that little bird in my hands I could feel its heart beating so hard from its fear of me. To that little bird that could not fly, I was big and strong, but I am not big, I am not strong, I am not intelligent. I am twenty years old now, but I am still a child. I have never even kissed a man. I would like to kiss someone, I would like to know what it feels like, but I am like that bird, I am scared.

I do not understand how hope works or where it can be found, so how can I have hope? How can I have courage? All I have is fear, and now in the foundation they have made more new rules for us to fear.

My housemother caught me wearing shorts in my room and she got mad and I got into trouble again. These days I am always in trouble coz of the new rules. I protest. All the co-daughters are protesting coz they have nothing to do and are bored. The rules are making big problems for everybody. The counsellors support us. They think the new rules are not necessary, but the board does not agree so all the counsellors have resigned. Ate Corandel, ate Josellee and ate Lollatonta all left the foundation and now there are no counsellors except ate Lollatonta. She left, but when she found out there was no-one to help us she said she would return and stay for two months until they find some replacements.

Now there is nothing to do and only one counsellor, so Princess and I make an agreement to ask ate Lollatonta if we can leave the foundation early. It is October and I have been here for almost five years. I can stay till the end of school semester in March, but what is the point. I do not want to go home. I want to go somewhere else, anywhere else, but there is nowhere to go. I feel helpless and unloved here. I feel like Father Mark and the housemothers are pushing me out of my safety place into a jungle full of evil animals like my uncle. But I also feel like it doesn't matter if I stay or leave coz now animal have entered the foundation wither their new rules to chase me away. I have to return to the jungle soon anyway, there is no alternative.

I can see no good in my future, no good family, no food, no study and no safety. I have no money and no help to go anywhere. If there was somewhere to go after the foundation I would never leave early, but there is nowhere to go and now there is no help or love for me here so it makes no difference if I stay or go. Sometime the foundation does find foster homes for the daughters, but there have been no foster homes for any girl leaving this year, all have been returned to their homes and many are in danger again.

Another reason I don't like to stay now is because our new social worker tells me I am a bad influence on my co daughters. I never do bad things that hurt anybody. Sometimes I do bad things like having a cell phone or jumping the wall or wearing shorts, and now I have a new long distance boyfriend on Face Book. He is a foreigner and he wants to meet me. Yes I do things like this, but these are not bad, they are just things to do coz now there is no TV and nothing to fill our time.

When the new social worker says I am a bad influence I don't know what to feel. All the time I try to make the daughters happy and laugh, this is gregarious. Father Mark told me I am gregarious so I looked it up and it says 'friendly and sociable.' How can that be a bad influence? There is so much sadness in the minds of us co-daughters that I think it is good to be gregarious and make people laugh and happy. But I think the real reason she said this is coz she went onto my FB and saw that I have communication with a foreigner man. He is a nurse and he works in a hospital near Perth in Australia, but sometimes he lives in CDO. He was married to a Filipina lady and has two children here, but they separated coz when he was away working in Australia his wife got pregnant to another man. Our new social worker sent him a message, but he didn't know her so he messaged me and asked, 'do you know this girl?'

'Yes' I say. 'She is a new social worker in the foundation.'

Our new social worker is twenty years old. Her name is Lexelle. She is the same age as me and I don't like this. She is not old enough to understand about the empty feelings that fill my inside or the bad things that happened to me. How can she advise us co-daughters when she has never woken up in the night whimpering in fear because an evil rapists is creeping into her mind. She cannot understand how us daughters feel.

The housemother says our social worker is a good role-model to us, but I asked, 'how can she be a good model if she wears shorts when she is going outside, but we are not allowed to wear shorts even in our rooms? What do you think? Do you think she is a good role-model when she does not obey the same rules that we must obey?'

When I say this the housemother gets mad, but she never answers me.

One night our new social worker slept in a hotel. I think she was with her boyfriend, but I am not sure of this, when she came back she had some cards from the hotel with all the prices of the rooms and she gave it to Indayjo and Yana and some of the girls. This cannot be a good role model, no way.

* * * * *

For a long time now I have been telling Father Mark that I am growing and my uniform is too small, that I need another uniform, so when all the daughters are having a meeting with Father Mark I ask again.

'Why don't you buy your own uniform?' he replies.

Everybody looks at me and for a minute I am so shocked I am speechless. 'How can I buy my own uniform? I have no money,' I eventually reply.

'You have a new boyfriend and he is a foreigner, so you have lots of money.'

I feel my face go as red as squashed watermelon. My mind is shocked and embarrassed at his words that my mouth is hanging open and my tongue won't move to reply. His voice hold the reproach of someone who believes that no end justifies the means and I should never take steps that are against the rules no matter how desperate the situation is, but the rules of the foundation are not the rules of life outside these walls.

While he is on his way to his car I stop him so we can talk alone and I explain. 'I do not have a foreign boyfriend. He is only a friend I chat to on Face Book. I did meet him once after class and we had a mango shake in Jollibee. We talked for awhile, but he is not a boyfriend and I would never ask money of him.' Then I say, 'anyway, it is the responsibility of the foundation to get me a uniform.'

Father Mark smiles when I say this. 'Relax,' he says. 'I'm not mad at you.' then he asks, 'Why are you mad at me?'

Does he need to ask me this? Doesn't he know? 'Because you said that thing to me about my friend in front of my co-daughters and you made me very embarrassed.'

He smiles then and goes to his car without saying anything more.

There are wounds in all relationships and now Father Mark is wounding me with his rebuke and his silence. *Ningas Cogon* comes to mind. It is a saying in the Philippines that means 'things start off well, but the good never lasts.' It is now clear that they don't want me in the foundation anymore and they are trying to get rid of me. I tell my counsellor that I will leave, coz even if my body is safe here, it is becoming a blackness place for my mind so *bahala na* - come what may, it does not matter if I am here or at the blackness place of my parents.

Sometimes I think there are two layers to me, one made of fear and tears, and another that wants more but is drowning so far beneath the fear and the tears that it cannot struggle to the surface. I cannot understand why or where my happiness has gone. I had happiness when I was young, then I knew nothing about being scared. What did I do that was so wrong that it caused my happiness to be been taken away? When I see life on television I know that happiness exists, but the happy lives of people on television does not exist for me. I have nobody who cares for me or helps me. In the foundation they have helped me for a while, but now they have turned against me and are going to send me back to that darkness place. There is nothing for me here in the foundation and nothing for me there at home, no friends, no loving family, no food, no education, nothing to do, no life anymore, only darkness and poverty and danger and fear.

I am leaving, but Princess has talked to the counsellor and decided to stay until she finishes her time in five months.

For my graduation from the foundation everyone makes a plan to go on an outing in the bush at Enitao. There is a zip line there and we can have fun playing on the hanging bridge in the trees, but at the last minute it is cancelled coz of a rainstorm. Instead we go to the cinema. Some of the movies we can't get into coz all the tickets are sold out. We settle for 'Gravity'. It is a science fiction movie about people being trapped in a space capsule. All the men die, but the only girl in the movie is saved because one of the men in the spaceship, who has died, appears in a dream and tells her how to save herself. She has someone who cares for her and looks after her even after he is dead. Her future is not sold out. After the movie we go to Jollibee and snack on burgers, French fries and coke floats before returning to the foundation.

Next day there is a party for my goodbye and I get a big surprise. All the girls give me something to remember them. Indayjo gives me a small drinking glass, I get a smiling face from Jelissa, a shell from Zelmarie, and Father Mark gives me a necklace with a cross. The girls make me a card and on the front they write on it.

> *'You deserve to be happier than you are*
> *because you make us so happy.'*

I cannot help it, I cry when I they give me this coz I feel so special. Many girls have left the foundation since I came, but never have the girls given gifts to anyone when they leave. I get so many things I have to ask …

'Why are you giving me these gifts?'

Father Mark answers for everyone. He says 'because you are very special. Everyone feels very close to you because you joke with everybody and make everybody laugh all the time.'

I like to make people laugh, their laughter does for me what Sunday mass does for people of religion, it makes me feel good inside, but I have never told anyone the reason why I try so hard to make then laugh. It is because for a short time their laughter fills the cavern of loneliness inside me. Sometimes I laugh out loud just for me, but my laughter sounds lonely when there is nobody to share it.

After the gift giving we celebrate with *chicharon* and ice cream and cake and bread and sweets and many other delicious things. I hug everybody and we laugh and cry together, but at night when I pack my things my emotions are in great confusion. I am sad to be leaving, the co-daughters are my friends, they are my family now and I will miss them. I am excited to be leaving, but I am scared also, coz I don't know what will happen in my home in Upper Biliran. I know I will not be able to continue college and I don't know what will happen to me or what I will do every day. I have no money, my family has no money, I feel I get no love or protection from my family and there is nobody to help me. All I can think is, one life is finishing and another is about to begin. I am at the end of a path I never expected to travel and I am about to embark on another one, but I am not the same person I was when I arrived here. The foundation has protected me for awhile, taught me a lot and given me some experience. It has put me at the beginning of a new life, maybe the one that will eventually lead me to a place where I feel safe and loved.

The date is October 31st 2013 there are twenty three girls in the foundation. In the morning the housemother checks my things and we have breakfast. She gives back the phone she confiscated and we wait for the counsellor who will accompany me home. At 11-o-clock we leave.

When I walk through the gates the air feels fresh and I feel free. I don't know why I feel this way, maybe because now there are no rules to be followed, maybe I feel free because I must accept my fate and look after myself. I don't know what will happen, but I am determined to make something of myself and to somehow live a good and open life. No longer will I hide from life.

We pass the church where the dead bodies lay when I went home after typhoon Sendong. The bodies are gone now and so has my safety. Part of me lies where they once lay. My life until now has been short, but already I have died many times. My happiness died when my uncle raped me. My mind died when my nun auntie and my mother wouldn't believe what my uncle did. I died from embarrassment when I looked in the eyes of my friends and saw how they judged me, and I died in the CR when I watched the blood drain from my wrist and I left it smeared on the mirror. I look at the scars that give character to my life, the gashes on my arm and wrist, and inside my right knee from carelessly wielding the *Sundang,* the burn from when I fell out of the guava tree into the fire, the scar inside my right inner arm from the infection when fell out of guava tree a second time, when I run my tongue over my teeth I can feel where the real ones finish and the false ones start, the scars on my wrist show the depths I plummeted when I fell into the pit of depression, each scar and bruise reminds me of how far I have come. Whatever will happen will happen, there is little I can do to control it. I am scared, but I feel happy, even if I don't understand anymore what happiness is.

Maybe now I am happy because I feel that nobody cares about me and I must look after myself. Maybe freedom is looking after yourself: Or maybe freedom is not caring what happens at all, coz if I don't care about anything, then nothing can hurt me. My thoughts about what is important have changed and my understanding of what freedom is has increased. Even if I cannot see it in my immediate future, I can now envision freedom. Maybe leaving the walls of the foundation has increased my freedom by allowing me the ability to see it.

I am nearing the end of this story, but really there is no end; the plot is still evolving. I am not really free coz I have no money, no job, no education, I have no family that cares for me and I have no innocence anymore. Sometimes I feel empty inside like there is a big hole where love should be, but with every hour and every kilometre I travel, the hurt is getting less.

In the foundation the counsellors took me to my past and if I can control my mind, I never want to go back there. My past is gone, now I can look to the future. Maybe it will be the most dangerous time in my life, surely it is the most unknown, but I will try to create my own tomorrow. and that tomorrow starts today. I will start it with a smile coz I feel like my mind is borrowing a little bit of happiness. I know it won't last. I know that if you borrow something you must pay it back, but until the next bad thing happens, freedom is the only thing I own for myself - it is mine. For the first time in my life I feel I can make a clear decision.

The end of this story is really the beginning.

Not all abuse victims find counselling, good friends and direction in life.

POST SCRIPT

On Saturday January 31st 2015, the Hall of justice where Irene was subject to so much influence by her nun Auntie, burnt to the ground killing two people.

On Friday 6th June 2015 Auntie Nona from Zamboanga died, aged 51, of complications arising from Diabetes.

EPILOGUE

March 2015

Irene

My journey is an old one for the world, but a new one for me, and for every girl who is raped. Fifteen months have passed since I left the foundation. I still hate my uncle, he is the devil. I cannot stop hating him. Even when I am happy his evil haunts my mind, but my life has changed. I met a foreign man who became my friend. I opened up to him and told him my story. He said he would like to write a book about my life, that it is an important story that should be told because it might help people to understand what girls go though when they suffer abuse. I offered him my diary.

At first I spent many hours interpreting it into English so he could understand it. This was very difficult because it hurt very deeply. It took nearly two months to do this because I did not like to read what I had written; I did not like to remember. We talked many times, for many hours, and many times I cried. This book is what he wrote as a result of reading my diary and those talks. The story is mine, although it has been formulated and told by my friend.

Trusting him was very hard at first, but when I got to know him, his words and advice gave me the opportunity to stop forgetting and start imagining. With his support I am now studying at Lourdes College in Cagayan de Oro. In a few years I hope to graduate so I can travel to work overseas in one of those tall buildings I dreamed about when I was young. Maybe this ability to look forward and see possibilities in the future is what Father Reno meant about hope.

I have friends now and I feel safe. I now share a pad together with ate Natasha. It is very small, only four metres by three metres and that includes the CR and the kitchen. When I stand in the middle of the room I can almost touch both walls. We have a portable gas cooker, but we don't use it much, gas is expensive. We have a rice cooker, so mostly we eat rice and some bully beef. I like our little place, it is secure and I feel safe here. Ate Natasha says I don't have so many nightmares now. My bad feelings are slowly going away.

Sometimes I think my life is very hard, but my friend says, 'If you believe your life is hard, it is. If you believe your life is good, it is. Whatever you believe is true. If you want to change your life, change what you believe.'

He is always saying things like this and trying to teach me about life. He says that I am much happier now than when we first met. He says that he burrowed so deeply into my mind that it is now showing specks of gold, but I am hiding them behind mistrust. It is hard to trust people. It is hard to believe any man, but my friend says not all people are like my uncle. When I try to look to the future however, I am haunted by the past. The worst part about the past is that you can never alter or change it. I wish I had been strong enough and had support to bring the case against my uncle and had him put in prison.

I have tried to read this story many times, but a strange feeling comes over me when I read about myself. The words make me feel like someone has peeled the clothes off my body and left me naked in a crowd. The words I read are such a true account of what happened and the way I felt at those times that when I try to read my story the feelings the words arouse in me are too raw, they are like a doctor who cuts too deep and removes all the goodness and leaves only the pain.

I do not expect anyone who has not had similar experiences of abuse to understand the pain that always haunts the mind of victims. Even when I am happy my laughter is a barrier to trust. I distrust people and I distrust happiness, I feel that happiness is like sunshine on a winter's day, it only remains until the next cloud comes along. One day I hope this will change and I can believe in people again. I hope that in the future I can find what happiness really is.

My friend calls me Little Lion because I am very small and my birthday is on July 31st, so I am a Leo. I like this name, it gives me the strength to believe that one day I might grow up to be strong and sunshine and happy days will return to my life.

Although this book is about me, I have not read all the words written. I have tried many times, but it is too painful, too many memories flood my mind and tears blind the pages from me. I have read about typhoon Sendong, my graduation, and my crush on Mary Kate. I laugh at these, especially the part about Mary Kate. When I read about my feelings for her now, I feel shy and embarrassed. Some of the girls from the foundation have become lesbians. They are still my friends, but my inclinations are not like that.

Ate Natasha.

Ate Natasha was only in the foundation for one year. When she arrived she was already an honour student in her home town of Dipitan where she studied on a partial scholarship. She left the foundation early because she felt stymied by the immaturity of the other girls and did not think the foundation could help her intellectual growth.

During her fourth year of college Natasha got pregnant to her seafarer boyfriend, at five months she had an abortion. She did this because she was afraid that if she didn't, Father Mark would find out and terminate her financial support. Their financial support was the only way she could finish her studies. Ate Natasha was supported because Father Mark knows her family from

Dipitan where the priests have a seminary. She is still a favourite of father Mark. He says she is a role model for other daughters. What he doesn't know won't hurt him.

She has now graduated from College as a qualified high school teacher and is waiting to sit the Board of Education exam. Her mother works abroad as a carer in Morocco and is paying her board and food until she can start work. Working abroad to support family is a common way for parents to educate their children in the Philippines

Until recently, ate Natasha and I shared a room in a boarding house with Josierose, but one day when I was going to pee in the communal CR, the brother of the owner opened the door and he was holding a knife. He went away, but I started shaking all over and was very frightened. A few days later ate Natasha caught him peeping through a hole in the CR while Josierose was washing. We told the owner of the boarding house, but she said he is her brother and he has no-where else to go so he must stay there. We found a new place and moved, but the owner of the old boarding house would not give my bond back. My friend went to see her and after they talked she gave it back.

Natasha tells me I should face up to my past and confront my uncle, that this is the only way I will lose my fear. She did this with the policeman uncle who raped her. After she did, he apologised and she forgave him. She found peace from this. My friend said this sounds like a sensible thing for her to do, but he is unsure of what would happen in my case. He says my uncle's history is not one of someone who committed an isolated offence like in the case of Natasha. My uncle is a predator with a long history of sex related incidents and a history of stalking me, that to confront him might give him an excuse to renew regular contact and create more fear in me. He suggested that if I do confront him I should wait awhile until I am more emotionally stable and only do so in the presence of people I trust.

Father Vegas

Father Vegas is worried about me. He texts me all the time to says he thinks my friend has bad intentions toward me, but Father Vegas is a priest. He has a fixation about sexual intercourse being a sin when it is not within marriage, I think he is wrong. My friend is kind. We talk a lot, he helps me with my education and while he has been writing he has looked after me and never hurt me. When he is not making me remember my past we laugh a lot. Ate Natasha and Ita Lollatonta think I am very lucky he is helping me. I think so too. My new life is a dream. If it wasn't for him I would still be in Upper Biliran with my family and be scared and in danger all the time.

Father Vegas is my second father, but really he is more like a father to me than my real one. Whenever he is in CDO we meet and he hugs me. He is so big that in his arms I feel like a little doll. He also makes me feel safe.

When they met, my friend asked him why some of the girls who leave the foundation get help from the priests to continue their education and some cannot. Father Vegas says he doesn't know what happens now, but when he was in the foundation he put rules in place for this. Firstly the girls must fulfil their full five years. Second they must have the academic potential to graduate from college. Thirdly, they must be of good moral standing. Lastly, that they have some means to provide board and food for themselves while studying, because the priest's help is for tuition only. Father Vegas said that he admits some girls fall through the cracks, that the foundation and the priests do what they can and he realises the inadequacies of the system, 'but,' he said, 'what else can we do? It is not possible to help everyone and not everyone takes advantage of help that is given.' He said that one of the ex-daughters came to him, she was covered with bruises because her boyfriend beat her. She said he did it all the time.

'Why don't you leave him?' he asked.

She said that she has nowhere to go and that 'at least with him I have somebody.' Father Reno said, 'When she told me this it broke my heart.' When he was telling us this story the pain in Father Vegas' eyes was easy to see.

Father Vegas acts like my father. He asked my friend if we are sexing each other and if we are going to get married. My friend told him no. He said he has no intention of marrying me and that anyway, he believes that marriage is just a piece of paper. Father Vegas got upset when he said that.

'My belief is different.' he replied.

Later my friend told me that everybody needs something to believe in and Father Vegas is no different. He has the right to believe anything he wants, but we live in an age of reason and the god of Father Vegas is an enduring myth, a bit like the Roman and Greek gods whose stories linger long after the rule of their civilisations have diminished their legitimacy. I know about some of the Greek and Roman gods, I study them in my English course in college. I also know that a myth is a belief from the past, but I don't really understand what he means when he says God is a myth. I know God from the lessons in the foundation, but I do not think God knows everybody, I do not think God knows me.

Ita Lollatonta

Ita Lollatonta is not my counsellor now, she is my friend. I call her *Tita,* in our language it means auntie. Sometimes she is still my counsellor when I need help or advice. Now she works as the Quality Assurance Co-coordinator at a major college in CDO and sits on the board of the Bitoon Sa Langit Foundation.

Father Mark

Father Mark apologised for hugging and kissing me. He said he saw how much the daughters loved Father

Vegas and wanted them to feel the same about him, so he tried to imitate what Father Vegas does. It was a mistake. Father Vegas is a foreigner and he hugs and kisses everyone. From the first time you meet him Father Vegas does this and he laughs and makes it fun. The daughters accept his kisses because they know there is no harm. Father Mark is a Filipino and all the girls know that when a Filipino man hugs and kisses a girl it is because he wants to sex them. He made a mistake, but now I understand why he did it Father Mark is my friend again. He is kind to us daughters. Sometimes he helps the girls if they are in trouble, even when they have left the foundation. I still have the chain and cross he gave me when I left the foundation. It is very special to me.

Josierose

Josierose is now at Cagayan de Oro College studying criminology. She was raped by her father and her grandfather. She brought a case against them and won. Her grandfather is dead now, her father is in prison in Davao. Her social worker at the applied for compensation and she got a large amount of money to support herself.

She has a boyfriend who is also studying criminology, but ate Natasha and I don't like him. When we were living with Josierose he would always hang around the room, lying on the bed and wanting Josierose to be on the bed with him. It is not nice to do this in front of other people.

Her college tuition is provided by the priests. She hopes to graduate in 2017, but there is a problem. She gave all her compensation money to her mother and stepfather and they spent it, now she has no money to pay for her board and food while she studies. She thinks she will have to go back to Butuan so she can live at home and study there.

Indayjo

Indayjo is sixteen now, but she is small and very immature. Her father was the one who abused her. When she went to the foundation he took the family and ran away and nobody knows where they are. She has only one year left in the foundation, but when she leaves she has nowhere to go. Indayjo has an uncle who might help, but she is afraid of him. Ate Natasha said that if she passes the Education Board exam and gets a job, and if the priests will pay for Indayjo's tuition, she would like to support her through college. My friend asked if Indayjo has the ability to graduate. Ate Natasha smiled at this question. 'She is lazy,' she replies, 'but maybe if someone helps her she will improve.'

Princess

In 2014 Princess graduated from College as Associate of Office Administration. She returned to Medina and is now pregnant and living with her boyfriend.

Gloryjo

Gloryjo studied in college in for six months while in the foundation, but after leaving she got no support. She works as saleslady in a clothes shop.

Gayfloreen

Gayfloreen returned to her home on the Dinagat Islands. She is now five months pregnant and living with her Muslim boyfriend who says he cannot marry her because she is not a Muslim.

Yana

Yana earned money by finding many sex friends who paid her. Sometimes she would go to the shipyards and sleep with the sailors to earn money. Several times she caught sexual diseases. The first time it happened she didn't have the money to go to the doctor or buy medicine so Natasha and I took her to the doctor. When my friend told the doctor that Yana was from the Bitoon Sa Langit Foundation and explained that all the girls were giving whatever they could to help her, the doctor was understanding and treated her for free. Some of us girls and Father Mark gave Yana money to buy the medicine to get better. She hasn't had her menstruation for three months and suspects she is pregnant. I suspect she doesn't know who the father is. She also has a large growth in her stomach. The doctor told her it is from a sexual disease she has had for several years.

Gennot

Gennot is studying social work and living in the boarding house with Yana, but she created a problem for herself. When she left the foundation the priests supported her tuition in college until she found a foreign boyfriend from Switzerland. He wanted her to go to Manila with him so she went She then wrote a letter to the housemother saying that the foundation never really helped her. When the priests read the letter and found out she went away with her boyfriend they stopped paying her college tuition. She thought her boyfriend would pay for her, but he said no. She is back in college now. I see her sometimes, but she doesn't talk to me. Her classmates say she is always talking about her boyfriend and showing them messages about what they do when they are sexing each other.

I don't like Gennot. When she shows people messages like this she shows no respect for herself. Also I didn't like her sending a letter like that to the housemother. The foundation was very good to me. They cared for me, they gave me counselling and protected me, they fed me, taught me manners, and for awhile they helped me get an education. I made many friends there and still have those friends. I did not always like the housemothers at the time, but I will always be very grateful to them, and the social workers, the counsellors, the priests and everyone who helped support us daughters.

Shiela

I see Shiela sometimes in *barangay* Carmen. She dresses very sexy and shows off her stomach and cleavage like a prostitute. Some of the girls tell me that she goes with boys and girls and anyone who wants her. Maybe she is confused and searching for love in the wrong places, but I think she is not a nice girl now.

Ate Noelene

Ate Noelene was one of the eight girls who left the foundation the March after I arrived. She completed a college degree in criminology and had just graduated law at a university in Cebu. I knew her only a short time, but we are very similar. When we are together we laugh all the time and are good friends.

Zelmarie

Zelmarie graduated from college with Ate Natasha, but she is still living in the foundation with seven other daughters. I saw her today and gave her some of my old clothes to give to the co-daughters. I did this because she told me that another daughter just arrived in the foundation and she is only seven years old and has no clothes. I cannot understand how men can rape the life away from anybody, especially a seven year old child.

The government should castrate them for this crime so they can never do it again.

Chemai

The reason Chemai came to the foundation must have been very bad. Whenever I ask her about it she never answers. She is still in the foundation and studying in elementary school. We meet at Ayala Mall sometimes if she has free time after class, or when I visit the foundation.

The foundation

I am told that things are different there now, Father Mark is in charge, he is Indonesian and very strict. There are more new rules that make the girls act like nuns. They must pray all the time and wear their dresses below the knees. One time when I visited them the housemother told me off, she said I was a bad influence on the girls because my T-shirt had some mesh at the back and showed some of my bra strap.

When I told this to my friend he said, 'give me the boy and I will give you the man.' He said this is a quote is from St Ignatius Loyola who founded the Jesuits order of Christianity. He explained, 'in the foundation they are using the stick instead of the carrot.' I didn't understand, so he explained further.

'To truly influence a person you must create a desire in that person to act for their own personal reasons.

You do this by placing something both you and they desire, in front of them, and give them the opportunity to achieve it. It makes them want what you want, this is the carrot. The saying comes from holding a carrot in front of a stubborn donkey so he will chase the carrot and pull your cart for you. When you get where you want to go you give the donkey the carrot and both get what you want. The alternative is to force someone to do what you want by using harsh rules or a stick to smack them with until they do what you want. This will work for awhile, but if your goal is not aligned with their desire, then when you stop beating them, they will stop doing what you want. The stick only works temporarily until the person being beaten rebels or is set free.'

I think he is right. In the foundation they make us go to church and pray all the time and do many things we don't want to. The girls resent this so when they leave, most do not continue doing the things they were forced to do.

After four years Chemai was expelled from the foundation and sent home for being caught with a cell phone. I am very sad for her. I am told the cell phone rule is to force the daughters to focus on their studies and protect them from outside influences like boyfriends, but it seems extremely harsh to send a young girl back into a dangerous situation just because she has a cell phone. Now all social media sites like Face Book and Twitter are blocked from the foundation computers.

I asked my friend what he thought about this. He said that it seems like the foundation has lost sight of its objective to protect and counsel the girls and to give them time to mature and overcome their trauma and find a direction in life. He said they seem to be focusing on their own religious agenda to the detriment of the girls. He also said that it is very difficult to argue against using such draconian measures because they can easily be argued to be in the moral interest of the girls. It depends on whether you take a religious or social point of view. He says that their methods will work in the short term, because most girls will fear being sent home, but when they leave, most will probably rebel against the imposed morality of coercion.

Irene

I am afraid to visit my home, I don't feel safe there. My parents and cousins always ask for money. They think that if have a foreign friend and I am in college I must have money. They don't understand that I have no money.

Last Christmas I went to Aurora to spend the semester break with auntie Nona. She treated me very nice, but my cousins there also asked for money to buy beer, so I came back to CDO and spent Christmas alone in the boarding house until college started again. It was lonely, but I thought about my life and what makes me, me. I wondered where I would be if I had stayed in Aurora with my auntie Nona when I was young. I think my life would be very different. Maybe I would have an education and a job, maybe I would be happily married, but maybe I would be like my sister or my cousin and have many children, no money and not enough to eat because my boyfriend or husband left me.

I do not regret what happened to me. It changed my life forever, but in a strange way it has given me a new future. When I compare my life now to where I came from, or what it was like when I was growing up, or when my uncle was abusing me, I cannot believe how much better it is. I am still afraid, but my fear is not so bad now that I can study and make new friends. My fellow students are becoming friends, but they have no idea what happened to me. I cover my feelings and hide behind laughter. Recently the teacher asked everyone 'what is the worst thing that has ever happened to you?' When it came to my turn I said, 'trauma.'

My classmates all looked at me. They were surprised because I am always laughing so much. 'What trauma?' they asked.

I could not tell them, they would never understand, so again I hid behind laughter. I wish my life had been different. I wish I had taken auntie Nona's advice and stayed with her. If I did I would now be graduated and might be working in a bank in Manila like a cousin that she also took in, but I have learned to live without regrets. Now my greatest fear is that I will wake one morning to find myself back in Upper Biliran and this life is only a dream. Life is good now, but I am still bothered by family. An auntie text to say her brother is in the hospital because someone stabbed him in the kidney and neck with a bamboo knife. She asked for money to pay for his expenses. After school I went to visit him and while I was in the hospital another auntie text to ask if I will buy a birthday cake for my grandfather. Even if I had the money I would not do this. I will never buy a cake to celebrate anything with the grandfather on my father's side, he is not listed in the good memories of my past.

My auntie does not know everything that happened to me. My counsellor, even my friend who wrote this book does not know everything that happened. Maybe nobody will ever know the story of all the other people who tried to sex me. I think it is best if some stay hidden. All the family on my father's side are evil, only my father is good. He beat me and he does not love me, but he is a good man.

My uncle found me again. He saw on Face Book that I have a foreign friend, so he got my phone number and is asking for money. I have changed my number so many times that now I cannot even give it to my family. I hate him. If there is one thing in my life I regret it is that he got away with what he did. I blame my nun auntie for this. She made me feel like a bad person and that what happened was my fault. She influenced me to not bring the case against him. I live with the fear that one day he will find me or that I will see him in the street, if this happened I don't know what I would do.

If I could advise any girl in the similar position to me it would be that, if you want to live your life without fear, be strong and bring the case against your abuser. No matter what the short term cost, it will help give you peace of mind in the long run.

I struggle with my lessons. They are hard to understand, but I am confident now to talk in front of the class. I learned that preparation is the key to confidence. My grades are improving and I will try my very best to graduate and make a good life for myself. It is hard to believe how much my life has changed and how lucky I am now. I hope I am not dreaming, but if I am dreaming, I hope I never wake up.